Tackle Climbing

Tackle Climbing
John Disley

Stanley Paul, London

The author would like to thank E. D. Lacey and Mervyn Rees
for permission to use photographs of which they own the
copyright

Stanley Paul & Co Ltd
3 Fitzroy Square, London W1

An imprint of the Hutchinson Publishing Group

London Melbourne Sydney Auckland
Wellington Johannesburg and agencies
throughout the world

First published 1959
Second impression 1961
Third impression August 1968
Revised edition May 1977
© John Disley 1959, 1977

Printed in Great Britain by litho at The Anchor Press Ltd
and bound by Wm Brendon & Son Ltd
both of Tiptree, Essex

ISBN 0 09 129270 0 (cased)
     0 09 129271 9 (paper)

Contents

1 Learning the Hard Way

We were in a motor-coach, a general air of festivity could be felt all around, an atmosphere for which even the fresh spring morning couldn't take the full credit. For wasn't this a Wednesday, a mid-week schoolday? A day when normally we should have been crouched over a dull textbook, half-listening to the drone of the master at the front of the room and the distant cries of those luckier than we on the games field. Instead we were inside a hired bus chugging along sixty miles away from the half-Welsh, half-English market town of Oswestry where our school was situated. Our destination was the summit of a Welsh mountain, Cader Idris – a 2927-foot/893-metre peak that dominates the collar of land between the Dovey and the Mawddach estuaries.

I was then fifteen years old and along with twenty-five other senior boys from school and several masters was engaged in furthering my geographical knowledge by an expedition. We were to be put down from the bus at Tal-y-Llyn, climb from the lake northwards over the main summit called Pen-y-Gader and then down the other side towards Dolgellau where the bus would meet us again. This would be a journey of about eight miles/thirteen kilometres, involving 3000 feet/1000 metres or so of uphill work, for the route meant losing height several times to reach various points. Not a fire-eating walk, but a good solid day out, especially for our novice party. Like all well-run expeditions we had spent some time prior to our departure preparing our plans.

7

In fact, several geography lessons had been devoted to the affair. We knew, in theory anyway, what kind of fauna and flora to expect to see and hear, what rock formations we would scramble over and what landmarks we would see from the summit cairn. We were also informed as to what deadly penalty awaited any of us who deviated from the straight and narrow path nominated by the expedition leader! It appeared that if our necks were not broken by the inevitable fall over the ever-welcoming cliffs, our geography master would kindly correct this omission when he caught up with us.

As our bus made its way over the high plateau of Montgomery from Welshpool to Cross Foxes we caught our first sight of the Cader Idris range. As we approached from the east the rock buttresses and cwms of the main cliffs were seen in the early morning sunlight, but even in the bright rays of the sun the cliffs remained dark and sombre, shaded now and then by large cumulus clouds that hung around the highest points.

We arrived at our destination and sorted ourselves out on the grass at the side of the road. We made sure that we had our maps with us, not real ones but diagrams drawn at school, and even more important we checked that our sandwiches were in our pockets. The party soon spread out along the path that runs across meadows into pine woods that flank the lower slopes of the mountain. Out of the trees we scrambled up the side of – and sometimes in – a cascading trout-stream that marks the side valley that we were using to gain the great basin of Cwm Cau, around which the main cliffs of the mountain towered. Before we had reached Llyn Cau the all-too-bright morning changed to a grey misty forenoon, and by the time we were gathered on the shores of the lake it was raining hard. We made a halt and the staff conferred while we waited for the stragglers.

Already the ring of cliffs around us was disappearing in cloud and rumour had it that the staff would soon issue a statement. We thought that the majority of the masters were for going back down before they, and even perhaps we,

Figure 1 The traverse of Cader Idris.

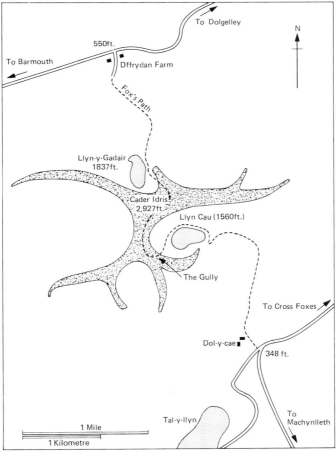

9

caught pneumonia. With this in mind five of us, determined not to be turned back after coming so far, drifted away from the main group. Carefully we wandered off until we were just out of earshot, and then, still as casually as we could, made for a gully at the back of the cwm. We climbed quickly for a few hundred feet and sat back, huddled in our raincoats, to await developments.

As we had expected we were soon missed and shouted instructions failed to reach us. Then to our joy the party, instead of moving back down the stream, turned towards the cliffs and started to climb to the ridge away to our right. It seemed as if our plan had worked for the path they were following was obviously the easy route to the ridge which our own gully would soon lead to. The authorities, presented with a *fait accompli* by our splinter group, had had to change their plans and follow us to the top and over the other side. We watched the small figures picking their way through the rocks below us and then we turned and pressed on up our choice of route.

The gully, easy and even grassy lower down, now steepened and became strewn with rock-rubble. Soon the walls narrowed and we were using our hands to pull ourselves over ledges of solid rock. We progressed slowly from ledge to ledge, keeping close together. Suddenly, just as we were about to tackle a slight overhang made by a large jammed boulder, a great crashing noise accompanied by a bouncing rock scared the living daylight out of us. We crouched under the edge of rock and watched stones the size of dog kennels whistling and ricocheting down our gully. Clouds of sparks cascaded from the rocks every time a boulder struck the side of the walls, and the smell of sulphur filled the dank air. Between falls we shouted out trying to indicate our presence to those above who we believed were responsible for the falls. We thought that the rest of the party had reached a point above our gully on the main ridge and were doing some 'trundling' thinking that nothing living was below them. How right they nearly were.

Actually we never really found out if the falls were 'boy-made' or natural, for none of our school party would admit to doing the silly act. Perhaps the culprits were too ashamed to own up, or perhaps it was just the rain and wind that had loosened blocks of rock and started the avalanche. Whatever it was that had started it finally gave up, and after waiting for a clear five minutes we emerged like frightened rabbits from our burrow. From then on we climbed with one ear cocked for warning of further stone-falls and one eye estimating the number of bounds needed to get our fragile bodies beneath a protective overhang.

There were no more fusillades and although the gully became looser and steeper we were never faced with an insoluble step. At last we reached the top and stood abreast the ridge, thankful to be there. It was raining hard – we could see nothing. To our left the ridge disappeared down into cloud; to our right it curved up out of sight. Not a soul was to be seen. We shouted – no reply, not even an echo. We had a hasty meeting and decided that the rest of the party had gone on over and past this point towards the top, and so we decided to follow them. Glad to be out of that gully we cheered up; the wetter we got the louder we laughed. My cousin's shoes – new that day – had begun to fall to pieces, dye from his red socks oozed out of the lace holes every time he bent his foot. The rest of us, happy in our Cadet Force boots, laughed at his plight, although to tell the truth our feet were little drier than his. Our only advantage was that the water in our boots stayed there longer and so our feet were slightly warmer than his, with his 'water-cooled' shoes.

We were now about 2300 feet/700 metres up and the wind

11

was making its presence felt. It would snatch open our rain-coats and lash a quick handful of rain at our shirts before we could gather the flapping material together. Our school caps, compulsory for the start from school but stuffed into a pocket soon after, were now gratefully pulled down over our heads, the peaks shielding our eyes from the driving rain. We followed a path marked by piles of stones called cairns. These were built about thirty yards/twenty-seven metres from each other and it was often difficult to pick out the next pile through the swirling cloud. Fortune favoured us and we finally reached the summit. The view we had been prepared for back at school was, of course, non-existent, but it was still a thrill to crouch in the lee of the summit and eat our soggy sandwiches. With nothing to see but grey-blue rock and sky and the wind cooling us off we didn't linger and set out down the Fox's Path.

We slithered down the glistening scree towards Llyn-y-Gadair, a small lake usually dark and quiet in its northern cwm. Today the wind pranced and leaped across the surface and then like some great grey bat lifted the tops of all the waves and climbed and swirled over the back of the cwm. Curtains of water moved horizontally from the llyn until they hit the screes around us. We could not be any wetter and our only consolation was that the rest of our party, still mysteriously ahead, were just as wet as we were. We pressed on down to the rendezvous with the bus, hoping that the others had waited for us. We reached the road at Dffrydan Farm.

There was no bus, no waiting party. At the farm we were told that we were the only people to come down off the mountain that day. So with little choice and tired legs, we set out for Dolgellau. Footsore and weary, not to mention our wetness, we limped the three miles/five kilometres into the small market town. As we entered the square, we were

A camping party consult the map during a trek across Exmoor. With loads of about 30 lb (14 kg), walking can still be pleasurable.

watched with amusement by the local people returning from work. There, to our relief, was the school bus outside a tea-shop. Our high spirits of several hours before when we had traversed the mountain had subsided on the walk along the road. Now they dropped right down. News that our expedition leader was exceeding angry cast a gloom over us. We crept into the café and awaited our sentence.

13

We were told, in no uncertain manner, that first, we were bigger fools than he thought us to be. Second, that we could expect no sympathy from him, or the rest of the staff, if we died from pneumonia, and third, that we, far from proving ourselves fine climbers, had broken a cardinal rule of mountaineering – that a party should always stay together, especially in bad weather. The ride home in the bus was a chill one, but even under the cloud of official disapproval a small warm glow in our middle refused to let us forget the thrill of reaching that summit cairn.

This was my first real lesson learnt on the mountains and, like so many lessons to follow, it was learnt with fortune favouring me. Tragedy could have so easily overwhelmed us in that gully, and there were many other occasions during the ascent and descent when a false path could have put us in a difficult position. In the future I was to remember that first rule of the mountains – never split up or leave slower members behind and – be glad that I had learnt it so easily.

After this initiation, wet and tiring as it was, I caught the climbing 'bug'. Fine week-ends would find me tramping over the local hills. Using my bicycle to reach the edge of the Berwyns and then walking over the summits in a wide circle would give me an excellent day out. I also discovered the Youth Hostels Association during this period, and whenever I had a couple of days free I would be off to the Snowdonia mountains. While staying at the hostels at Capel Curig, Idwal Cottage, or Llanberis I climbed most of the 3000-foot/900-metre mountains in Caernarvonshire. Bit by bit I learnt a little more about the art of mountaineering. I watched other climbers, noted what clothes they wore, how fast they walked, which way they tackled slopes. I read all the books on climbing that I could borrow from the public library and soon began to think that I knew all the answers.

It was at Easter 1947 that I found that things weren't quite as easy as I had thought, and I learnt another lesson.

I was now a student, and with two friends had decided to do a walking tour of the Lake District. Back at our base at Loughborough we sorted out our Youth Hostels and decided on our routes. We looked at maps and nominated the various high peaks that we would climb. We also set ourselves up with the equipment we should need. We bought rucksacks, converted raincoats into anoraks, and nailed army boots with clinker nails. This last operation took us a lot of time as the queer-shaped nails bent the wrong way more often than the right. We went on training walks and got ourselves as fit as we could, for we were determined to 'finish off' the Lakes in seven days.

After returning to our homes we made a rendezvous for one Easter morning at Kendal railway station. Instead of waiting for the connection that would take us on to Windermere, we decided to break ourselves in with a twelve-mile/ nineteen-kilometre walk over the Fells to Bowness and then on to the hostel at Troutbeck. Although our bodies stood up to the effort without strain, our precious boot-nailing suffered. We lost a grand total of thirty-seven nails, and decided on the spot to get the job done professionally next time. Helvellyn was our first major target, to be climbed from Grasmere Hostel. We walked up the road until we reached the end of Thirlmere, and there looked for the path that would lead us up to the long backbone that makes up the mountain. We stepped off the road not on to grass and rock but on to snow. At first it was only a sugar-coating we strode over, but as we climbed higher it became deeper. Visibility was still reasonable and although we could barely pick out the path it was fairly obvious in which direction we should go to reach the ridge.

The long back of Helvellyn, 3118 feet/950 metres high,

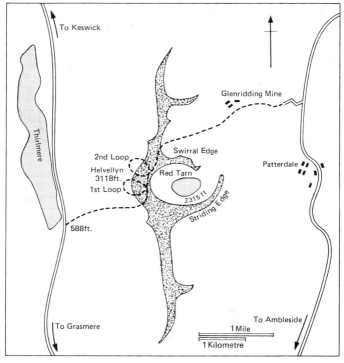

Figure 2 Lost on Helvellyn.

extends for nearly four miles/6·5 kilometres in a north to south direction. From its eastern side the famous ridges of Striding and Swirral Edge stick out like the arms of the letter K, but our side of the mountain was free from cliffs and made up of fairly steep slopes normally covered with grass. On that day we plodded up long snow slopes and as we climbed higher the clouds came lower. We met at about the 2250-foot/700-metre mark. Cloud doesn't suddenly arrive, it creeps up on you, gradually reduces visibility, until to your surprise you are alone in a little grey world. When we turned to mark our progress we were unable to see the road below us, but it didn't really worry us and we pressed on. It got darker and soon the cloud began to settle firmly around us. Snow started to fall and the wind began to blow. It is at this point that we should have recognized the danger signs – snow, wind and the start of a blizzard. We were, however, too proud to turn back, and although we didn't know the mountain we were sure that a path uphill would take us to the top and, conversely, a downhill one would bring us back to the road.

'We'll go on a bit further,' I said, 'it will be very simple to drop back down the slope when we have had enough of this snow.'

As luck would have it we came out at a large cairn from which the ground dropped down away from us.

'The Top,' we cried, and felt that our going on had been justified.

We ate our sandwiches in the little protection given from the wind by the cairn, and then set out to retrace our steps. The wind had long since blown our foot-marks away, but it was fairly obvious which was our way. We walked for about five minutes, and then, to our astonishment, a much larger cairn loomed up out of the snow. This was certainly not there on the route up and was moreover obviously the correct top of Helvellyn. We weren't exactly lost because we knew where we were, but which way was down?

'Right, now what?' asked my companions.

'Still as easy as pie,' I replied. 'If this is the top all we have to do is to walk westwards and the road will be reached over easy slopes.'

We set off into the wind which had been blowing to our backs on the way up. One behind the other we stumbled through the deep snow. The top of Helvellyn is like a plateau several hundred yards square, and there is little to

17

indicate at first which is the way down, as it is all fairly flat. After ten minutes, to our horror, we were back at the summit. We had walked in a large circle. Thoroughly frightened by now we tried again. We kept close together, our eyes straining to pick out easy slopes. Suddenly the white gloom ahead of us lightened, and there, in front of our feet, lay nothing. The steep cliffs which the map claimed were absent on the west side of Helvellyn were slap in front of us. Very scared we crept along the edge of the cliffs until we reached a spot where the slope was a little less than vertical.

Below us the snow slope disappeared into a whirling whiteness and for all we knew might have soon become an overhanging cliff. By now all we wanted was to get down out of that wind, and anything was preferable to that featureless summit plateau. We had eighty feet/twenty-five metres of hemp rope with us and we roped up. I lowered myself down for the length of the rope, made a hole to stand in, and shouted for the other two to join me. Although I was only forty feet/twelve metres below them I could not see them through the snow; after a few minutes I was joined by the others slipping and sliding down my tracks. In this fashion we made our precarious progress downwards. To our relief the slope slackened off and after about an hour, to our delight, we began to see things below us.

A valley opened up and although it was totally different from the one we had left that morning, it was as good as the 'promised land' to our snow-blinded eyes. We staggered across a snow-covered bog, climbed over a sheep wall or two and were standing on solid ground for the first time for nearly seven hours. At a small cottage we asked a very foolish question.

'Where are we please?'

We were told that we were in the Glenridding Valley, two miles/three kilometres above Patterdale village, right on the

Setting the map with a protractor compass during a Mountain Leadership Course in Wales.

east side of the mountain. We had come down over the very cliffs that we had made every effort to miss. So much for our route-finding by using the wind as a guide. When we reached the village we telephoned our Grasmere hostel to warn them that we would be late getting back. We had twelve miles/twenty kilometres to walk over the Kirkstone

Pass to reach Grasmere and plenty of time to realize what fools we had been.

We had under-estimated the mountain and been too cock-sure of our own ability to walk in a straight line. We had gone on blindly, taking no notice of the worsening weather, and only Fortune had been good to us and led us first to the summit and then to the one point on the eastern side where descent was possible.

For the rest of that Easter tour we were careful to keep below the snow-cloud level, and we checked each turn we made with a new compass that we had bought in Ambleside.

A strange mountain, however simple it may look on a map, becomes a formidable proposition in bad weather, especially if you try and traverse it without using a compass.

On this occasion I had remembered my first important lesson, and to our credit we had been careful to stick together. In future I was to remember the second points. Never under-estimate a mountain. And don't over-estimate your own judgement in preference to a map and compass.

2 Get Started Yourself

If you read a book on athletics, you will probably find several chapters devoted to the technique of running. In these pages you will be informed how to put your foot, where to put it, what to do with your arms, how to hold your head and when to breathe. In fact these instructions will baffle you with science. Actually there is only one important rule in running and that is: 'to be sure that you do not move the same leg twice in succession!' If you remember that the right foot always follows the left, and *vice versa*, then you have mastered the fundamentals of moving. All you now need to make you a better runner is lots and lots of practice.

The same applies to the technique of hill-walking. Many words can be written about it – few are really necessary. Just as in running where plenty of training will smooth off your action, so in hill-walking it is the same. The more you do of it the better you will become.

I remember an occasion while I was still at school when I was taken out for the day with a climber nearly four times my age. We were a party of six and the top of Snowdon was our destination. The five of us from school had cycled round to meet our guide at the head of the Llanberis Pass. We were staying at the Idwal Cottage Youth Hostel, and as we pushed our bikes up the last bit of hill that leads to the Pen-y-Pass Hotel we caught up our leader who had walked from Capel Curig five miles/eight kilometres away. Leaving our bikes in the car park we headed across the small field that leads to the Pyg Track. The Pyg Track is a medium difficult path, although much easier than the Horse-shoe Trail; it is much more interesting than the easier Miners Track or Llanberis Path. It starts at 1169 feet/356 metres above sea-level and then crosses a col to reach the inside of the Snowdon bowl, making its way by the Zig-zags to the summit (3561 ft/1085 m) (*see* map on page 54).

Once on the rough path we fell into single file and walked behind our guide. After several minutes we realized that he had over-estimated his strength, for the pace he was setting was funeral-like. Plod, plod he went, and behind him we young bloods fretted and chaffed at the slowness.

'He should have taken the bus from Capel Curig,' we muttered, 'he is tired out already.'

The path for the first few miles was obvious and as soon as we could we fled past our leader and raced on in front. This was more like it. We jumped from rock to rock, made great strides over boulders and used our arms to pull up over obstacles rather than detour round them. Because we were travelling fast, now and again we missed our footing and banged our toes and legs on protruding rocks. This meant that we had to have fairly frequent stops to inspect our injuries. On these occasions we would look back down the path for our guide. Luckily he still seemed to be moving up behind us although his slow plod had not changed even on the steep slope that we were now on.

After these brief stops we would shoot off again, hurling ourselves at the loose screes and scrambling over the heather-covered rocks. As the slope steepened and the sun got brighter we became hotter and before long we didn't always need the excuse of a slight accident to claim a short rest. In our hurry we missed the very obvious path occasionally and had to retrace our steps. It must have been about an hour after we had first left our leader and while we were strewn over the path having a breather that he suddenly overtook us

Even the decorative brickwork on the gable end of a school gymnasium can provide an opportunity to practise climbing. Low-level traverses are safe if exhausting.

'We'll have our first rest up at the col, lads,' he remarked, and on he plodded.

We fell in behind him; it was still the same pace, but now it seemed twice as fast as before and it was all we could do to stay with him. When we reached the col, we didn't have to be told about 'conservation of energy' or 'rhythmic movement'. We had found out for ourselves.

The rest of the day was an object lesson for us. We reached the summit and descended over Lliwedd back to Pen-y-Pass. Our guide, for all his years, was still using the same pace when he stepped back on to the road after some six hours of rough walking. He had to wait a while before he could say his 'goodbyes' to the party, because some of us were straggled a bit behind. He thanked us for our company, hoped that we had enjoyed the day and then set off jauntily towards Capel Curig. We were hard put to it to climb on our bicycles and thankful that the first four miles/6·5 kilometres home was downhill.

All professional walkers are economical in action, just as the champion runner is relaxed. Watch a hill-shepherd walking after his dogs, or a policeman pacing his beat, or even a tramp on the edge of the main road. All of them waste no energy by making flamboyant flings of the legs or waving of the arms. Neither do they appear to be hurrying – their stride is a comfortable one that brings them to the end of the day without undue fatigue or strain. They have achieved such perfection by lots of practice, and you will soon develop for yourselves that 'easy gait' that characterizes the accomplished hill-walker.

Remember these points:

1 Develop a personal rhythm.
2 Alter speed by lengthening the stride and keep rhythm the same.

3 Memorize the footholds three or four paces ahead.

4 Flex the knees or straighten to smooth out irregularities.

5 Place the foot flat wherever possible to get the best grip and avoid strain on the ankle.

6 Halts should be definite but not prolonged. They should be made where possible at natural stopping points: i.e. on top of ridges, before or after difficult sections, etc.

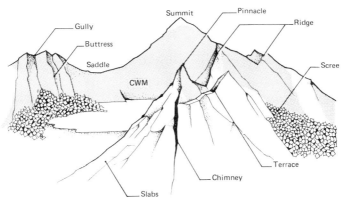

Figure 3 The features of a mountain.

As I spent more time in the hills I found that I needed certain equipment that was specialized and designed to protect me from blisters, bruises and the weather. There is, as I very soon found out, no better way of throwing your money down the drain than by purchasing equipment before you know what to look for in design and material.

I once bought by mail-order coupon, with a pound note that was burning a hole in my pocket, an ex-W.D. sleeping-bag. The makers claimed in their advertisement that it was 'exceptionally warm and water-proof'. Of this there was no doubt. When it arrived it took two strong men to carry it

25

Off to camp with high-loading sacks that are well balanced.

from the van to the front door. The immense kapok-lined bag was covered with a thick rubber-coated canvas. It would have been ideal for using in a fixed camp, where the gear was sent ahead by train, but for lightweight camping and bivouacking it was useless. I had wasted my heard-earned money. Since then I have seldom bought anything by mail-order, preferring to 'see the pig, rather than buy it in a poke'. Even honest descriptions of an article, and there are many that are not, can be misleading. Always try and see the piece of equipment you mean to buy. Try it on, test its strength, feel its weight and generally decide if it meets your needs.

Today there are so many firms manufacturing different types and models that it would be impossible for me to list every piece of equipment and note its virtues and faults. The best I can do is to point out the main function of each item needed for hill-walking. Then, if you add my advice to the first-hand experience that you will soon gather for yourself, you will be able to judge the probable efficiency of your intended buy.

Boots

First you will need to consider your feet. An army may 'march on its stomach', but the hill-walker will notice his feet long before his tummy complains of neglect.

Stout shoes might serve you for a few low-level walks and, if nothing else is available at first, then they will have to do. I have seen many parties walking on the Surrey Downs, or on the Chilterns, or even on Ben Nevis in high summer, in strong lace-up shoes. They were doing well, too, but were all sensibly keeping to the paths. Shoes, however, are just stop-gaps, especially if you wish to make your own way and leave the beaten tracks behind. For once you are off solid rock, you are struggling with loose scree, deep heather, jagged rocks or soggy moss. Ankles must then be protected, feet kept dry, and some form of cleating will be necessary to give your feet grip.

It is possible to spend a great deal of money on a pair of boots. Some hand-made Italian and English pairs cost as much as £25–£30. Obviously for this amount a near-perfect boot can be expected. At the other end of the scale there is the ex-army boot in various styles costing as little as £3. However, whatever you can afford to pay for a pair of boots there are certain basic points to look for when you buy them:

1 The leather should be of stout cowhide, fairly supple around the ankle but firm at the toes and heels.
2 Unless the quality is very good, the boots should be unlined. Linings often ruck up and give blisters.

27

3 The soles should project less than a quarter of an inch/ 6 mm from the uppers. This will help bring your actual foot as close to the rock as possible, and make your steps more accurate.

4 The tongues should be sewn in at the sides. This will help to keep the foot water-proof right up to the ankle.

5 Good strong tabs at the back. They will help you to pull the boots on when wet, and also hold the laces down on the boot when you have tied them round the top.

6 Boots should be tried on for size with one pair of thick socks or stockings. Look for plenty of room around the toes, so that wriggling is possible.

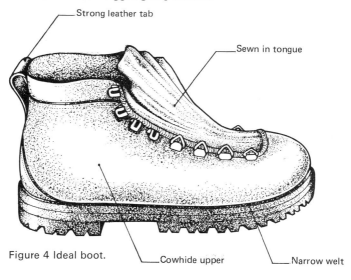

Figure 4 Ideal boot.

So much for the boot itself – now for the tricky problem of the sole. Up until the early 1950s nails, in one form or another, reigned supreme on the bottom of the boot. Since then moulded rubber has been developed to make a long-

Figure 5 Nails: Treble hob Star mugger Clinker Tricouni.

lasting sole for mountaineering boots, and the nails illustrated in Fig. 5 are seldom seen in the hills today. Rubber soles are first-class for tramping and rambling the hills particularly if lengths of road or lane are included in the day's march. The rubber cushions the foot and to coin a phrase from motoring parlance 'gives a quieter ride'. As long as the weather stays dry, all is well with the rubber sole. However, should it become wet, as indeed it often does in the U.K. mountains, then rubber has its disadvantages. British rock, surrounded and often covered with vegetation, becomes very greasy when it is wet, and rubber boots can slip as nicely as ice skates on a rink. Many good climbers have come to grief on a grass-slope damp with rain after climbing a steep rock-face.

The trick to staying upright in rubber boots on wet polished surfaces is to recognize instantly the loss of friction that water produces and to adapt your stride immediately. Similarly, on wet grass or vegetated rock or scree – take more care in selecting every footfall.

There are many mountaineers who recommend a partnership between rubber and nails as the best arrangement for general walking in the mountains. They have 'clinker' nails placed in the heels and this gives them the security they want when moving on wet rocky surfaces.

For interest you should know that there were two kinds of nails used for climbing boots in the era before rubber soles. Hob nails, star-muggers and clinker nails all worked on the principle that the rock was harder than the nail, and these nails were made of softish iron. The tricouni nail worked on the opposite idea and was made of steel so that it could bite into the rock and get a grip. The usual patterns of nailings are shown in Fig. 6. Tricouni nails were used for rock-climbing and the other nails for scrambling and hill-walking.

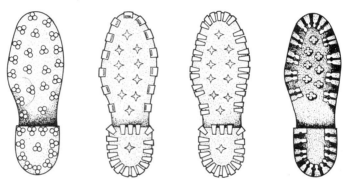

Figure 6 Hobs Clinkers Tricounis Vibram.

No matter how much or how little you pay for your boots they will be worth looking after. The following care should be taken:

Keep the leather well polished with ordinary shoe-polish.

After use brush the soles and seams free of grit. If the boots are wet, leave them to dry in a warm room, or outside in the air. Do not put them anywhere near a fire. I once lost a good pair of boots in a Welsh farmhouse oven. They came out dry all right, but also brittle, so that the next time I wore them the stitching parted and the leather cracked open.

Socks

Working upwards from the boots we come to the socks. These need to be thickish and long enough to reach well up out of the ankle of the boot. In the old days hand-knitted Harris-wool socks were considered to be the finest available, and there was also a strong opinion that insisted on two pairs of socks being worn.

Today, with better fitting boots, and new materials for socks, most mountaineers only wear one pair of medium thick socks in their boots. Wool is still very popular, but brushed nylon socks with loop-stitch are well thought of too, particularly as they dry faster and are less likely to wear into a hole than wool. These socks are available at mountain- and ski-equipment shops at about £1·25.

For starting off without additional expense, football stockings are as good as anything. But remember that you are going to feel every wrinkle in your socks and over several hours of walking a bad darn or a hole will probably give you a blister. Look after your socks and avoid trouble.

Trousers

Long trousers are essential for wearing in British mountainous country particularly if you intend going out in all sorts of weather and traversing the summits. An old pair of flannel trousers – wool and nylon mix – will be very suitable and provide good protective qualities.

There is still some ex-army clothing around that is cheap and very useful for climbing. The materials are usually very good but the cut and placement of pockets are not always as we should wish.

Blue jeans are not a success, for although the material is tough and light the legs are usually cut too tightly. This

31

leads to a drastic curtailment of lifting ability when the trousers get wet, as the material sticks to the skin.

A pair of trousers should be fairly loosely cut to give ample movement at the knee. With little technical skill at the sewing machine it is possible to modify a pair of old flannels to produce a very worth-while pair of climbing trousers.

1   Turn down the turn-ups, and if this makes the trousers too long, cut off the ends. Then taper the bottoms by turning the pants inside out and from a point six inches/15 cm below the knee machine the legs down to make the bottoms about six to seven inches/15–18 cm across.

2   Reinforce the seat and knees with strong patches. These will ensure that you get home 'decent' even after the wildest of walks.

Even in hot weather shorts are unsuitable in mountainous country. Scrambling through thick bracken and heather will soon draw blood on uncovered legs, while the roughness of the rocks will scrape the skin from the knees very quickly if they are unprotected. Shorts are fine for short-grass walks on the Chilterns or the Downs, but in the mountains, where the weather changes so suddenly, long trousers are the order of every day.

Anoraks

Next on the list comes the top of the body, a section which contains all the vital organs of the frame, and one it is essential to keep warm. Underneath the outside garment it is best to wear several layers of clothes. A string vest next to the skin, followed by a wool shirt and two light, long-sleeved, wool jerseys, will give you complete protection and heat insulation. Not only do the fibres of the material keep the warm air in, but the air between the layers will be trapped and act as insulators. It is these air-pockets which keep you warm. If you rely on one massive sweater, even if it is heavier than two lighter ones together, you will get poorer protection. Besides which you have only two variations of dress – on and off – while with several layers you can strip down a bit at a time. Wool is the best material to use, as it stays fairly fluffy even when wet, and so retains that valuable layer of air. Here again nylon fibre pile in its 'furry' form is used for jerseys and is well liked by mountaineers.

On top of all this you will need some form of 'anorak'. This is a smock-like garment evolved from the one worn by the Eskimo. Such a coat will keep out the wind and is made of a very close-weave material for this purpose. Do not expect your anorak to be rain-proof, for nothing short of rubber or plastic will keep out driving mountain rain for more than a few minutes. In any case, if the anorak is completely impermeable to air, like rubber or plastic would be, then you would soon be wet from condensation inside your clothes, even on fine days.

Rain is all part of the fun of climbing, and you must expect to get wet, but as long as you stay warm you will come to little harm even if you are soaking wet. So regard your anorak as a wind-proof garment only and don't be disappointed if it leaks. If it is imperative that you keep dry, then the best thing to wear is a large-size plastic raincoat big enough to go over your pack. A more 'professional' garment for overall protection is the 'cagoule' – a long hooded smock, free from openings and closures. They cost between £4 and £6 for a simple lightweight version in nylon. Generally speaking, the lighter the material, the less time you will have its use – and therefore heavier and perhaps more expensive cagoules and anoraks are cheaper in the long run.

Good anoraks cost anything from £7 to £16, depending

upon the material and workmanship. The main points to look for are:

1   A strong, close-weave or proofed material, i.e. cotton duck, bri-nylon, P.V.C.-coated cotton, gaberdine.

2   Roominess. Make sure that you have plenty of space in the arms and body when wearing several layers of jerseys.

3   Length. Ensure that the anorak reaches well down the thighs; nearly to the knees is fine. When you want to stay warm and dry you are not competing in a fashion show.

4   Reinforcements. Look for double-thickness material at the points of wear – elbows, cuffs and shoulders.

5   Good sensible pockets. Pockets need flaps to keep out the rain; they are even better with a zip or 'velcro' fastening too. The chest pocket should be large enough to take an O.S. map, compass and whistle (11 in × 8 in/28 cm × 20 cm).

6   Well-stitched seams all over the garment. There is more than one way of fastening two pieces of material together, and a 'plain' seam is not recommended for this vital piece of equipment. The best seams are 'taped' seams, but 'rolled' seams are good enough, especially if the garment is made so that no seams occur at potential leaky points, e.g. the shoulder tops.

7   Other refinements. A really efficient hood. These can be bought with wire in the seam so that the hood can be moulded like a peak. Sometimes you yourself can push some malleable wire into the seam and improve the hood.

Strong nylon zips, with overlap. Draw-cord at the waist and skirt. Inner-cuffs or closures at the sleeves. A distinctive colour – bright colours such as orange and yellow do stand out better in mist and poor light.

Other Equipment

All you need now to complete the picture of a well-equipped rambler in the hills is a woollen hat – with or without pom-pom on top. The traditional 'balaclava-helmet' still takes some beating at about £1·50. Also needed are woollen gloves or mitts.

Now you will be ready for any kind of mountain weather normally experienced from Easter to October in British hills.

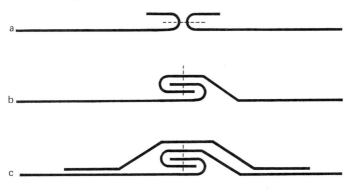

Figure 7 Types of seams. Seams are the weak points of any garment. The better the quality of the material the more elaborate the seam will be, as shown above: A Plain – easily pulled apart; B Rolled – long lasting and secure; C Rolled and taped – best waterproof quality.
N.B. The more thoughtfully a garment is designed and cut, the fewer seams will there be of any sort.

3 Where to Go

Just like 'All Gaul', which Caesar described as being 'divided into three parts', so is Britain divided with regard to mountaineering. We have the good parts, the better-than-nothing regions, and the flat-as-a-pancake areas.

For the most part all the good mountain-walking country is situated in the west of Britain. The better-than-nothing regions, by which I mean the hills of the Midlands and the South, fill in the centre portion of the map of England. The hopeless areas are found next to the East Coast. If you are unfortunate enough to live in Lincoln, Norfolk, Cambridge, Suffolk or Essex and want to climb regularly you will have to move. Go west, young man or girl.

Luckily, most of our main cities are fairly close to 'brown areas' on the map. Liverpool and Manchester have a regular Friday night exodus, west to Chester and north to Lancaster. On both these exit routes you will find the climber motoring, walking, cycling, or hitch-hiking to the hills. They will be trying to reach Capel Curig or Windermere before Saturday arrives. Sunday tea-time sees the traffic reverse its flow. Back to work on Monday morning is the hope now.

> I'm chained to the work-bench on Monday,
> I'm roped to the High-crags on Sunday

so the chorus goes of the 'Climber from Manchester Way'.

The mountaineers of Birmingham, Stoke-on-Trent and Wolverhampton find their way easily up Watling Street into

Practice with maps and compasses can be effective, even on the moderate slopes of the North Downs.

Wales, straight on through Llangollen to Snowdonia, or branching off at Oswestry for the Cader Idris range.

The Sheffield, Derby, Nottingham and Leeds climbers simply walk out of their front doors up the valleys of the Dove or the Derwent, straight into the Peak District, or the valleys of the Aire or the Wharfe to the central Pennines.

Tynesiders head west into the Cross Fell or Mickle Fell sections of the Pennines or up north-west into the Cheviots. Scots living in Glasgow or Edinburgh have the mighty Grampians within a few miles of their city boundaries.

Only London is difficult for access to the mountains. But even with nothing high or igneous at hand the Londoner is not completely plain-bound. A few miles south is the ridge of the North Downs curving from Guildford to Reigate. To the north are the Chilterns. Not very much perhaps – but height isn't everything and the Downs and the Chilterns despite their lack of feet can give fine training walks and good practice in map-reading. South-west of London the sandstone outcrops around Tunbridge Wells and East Grinstead even give opportunities for hard rock-climbing.

Where to go to climb is only half the problem – where to stay when you get there is the other half. If you are a novice climber just starting out into an area for the first time, you will want to be fairly mobile so as to be able to explore the ranges around your base. To help you do this I can give no better advice than to tell you to join the Youth Hostels Association. The Y.H.A. have nearly 300 hostels open for their members, and naturally enough there is a high concentration of these in the mountains. Membership is easy and cheap (*see* Chapter 9), food is nearly always available at the hostels, as is your bedding. By spending your nights in a Youth Hostel you will be able to get on with the expedition side of your holiday. The pack on your back will be small and you will not be handicapped by having to spend time every day visiting shops to buy food.

As you move about, either using one hostel as a base or travelling from one to another, keep your eyes open for signs of other accommodation. Mark on a map the farms which allow camping in their valley fields. Some farmers provide barns for ramblers to spend the night in – look out for these. When you are on the high hills you will probably see a few tents nestling in perfect sites, near to a stream and protected from the prevailing wind. Remember where these sites were. With all this information gathered from the security of the Youth Hostel booking, you can decide next time you visit that area whether to camp out on your own or not.

When you become more experienced in mountaineering and mountain camping, you will be able to set out for a strange region without a prior survey from the hostel. You will have developed an 'eye' for good camp-sites and friendly farmers. But to begin with use the Youth Hostels, for you will learn a great deal from them and make many friends.

The map on page 41 shows the twelve main groups of mountains and hills where most climbers do their mountaineering in this country. The following notes apply to these areas:

Usually called Snowdonia

Consists of three mountain ranges, separated by the passes of Llanberis and Nantffrancon.

1 The Snowdon Group – with three 3000-ft/914-m peaks.
2 The Glyders – with five 3000-ft/914-m peaks.
3 The Carnedds – with six 3000-ft/914-m peaks.

Best gateways: By train to Bangor or Bettws-y-coed.
By road up the A5 from Shrewsbury or Chester.

Youth Hostels at Capel Curig, Idwal Cottage, Llanberis, Snowdon Ranger, Bryn Gwynant, Pen-y-Pass, Roe-wen.

Initial Expeditions (suggested for the first visit to the area in summer conditions)
1 Ascent of Snowdon, 3561 feet/1085 metres. Highest mountain in England and Wales. Take the Pyg Track starting from the Pen-y-Pass Hotel.
2 Ascent of Tryfan, 3010 feet/917 metres. A rock peak. Climb by way of the Heather Terrace, starting at the tenth milestone (from Bangor) on the Ogwen lake-side.
3 Ascent of Carnedd Llewelyn, 3485 feet/1062 metres. Highest peak on the Carneddau. Start at Pont Rhyd-goch and climb by way of Ffynnon Llugwy and Pen-y-waun-wen.

More Ambitious Expeditions (good weather and experience needed)

1   The circuit of the Snowdon Horseshoe, with the knife-like Crib Goch ridge. Start and finish at Pen-y-Pass. Allow 5–6 hours.

2   Traverse of the Glyders. Start at Idwal Cottage Youth Hostel, climb up to Idwal Lake and then to the plateau above the Devil's Kitchen. Climb east over Glyder Fawr and Glyder Fach and down to Bwlch Tryfan.

3   A crossing of the Carneddau. Taking in six of the fourteen 3000 feet/914 m mountains in Wales. Start at Idwal Hostel and finish at Roe-wen Hostel.

The Berwyn Range

A remote and lonely area of valleys and ridges between Llangollen and Bala.

> Best gateways: By train to Llangollen or Bala.
>
> By road to Llanrhaiadr-ym-Mochnant, Llanarmon, Dyffryn Ceiriog or Llandrillo.

Youth Hostels at Llangollen, Cynwyd and Plas Rhiwae-dog.

Expeditions

Starting from the waterfall at Llanrhaiadr, a traverse of the ridge of Moel Sych to Cader Fronwen, descending south to Llanarmon or north to the Dee valley at Llandrillo.

Or, from the west end of Bala Lake, south over Aran Benllyn to Aran Mawddwy (2970 feet/905 metres, the highest Welsh mountain outside Snowdonia). Down to Dinas Mawddwy, or back to Bala via the famous Bwlch-y-Groes Pass.

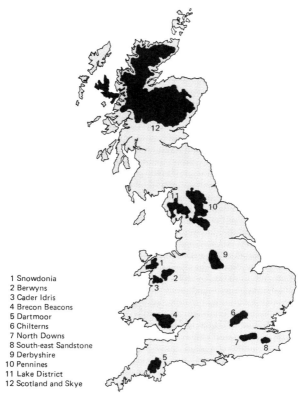

1 Snowdonia
2 Berwyns
3 Cader Idris
4 Brecon Beacons
5 Dartmoor
6 Chilterns
7 North Downs
8 South-east Sandstone
9 Derbyshire
10 Pennines
11 Lake District
12 Scotland and Skye

Figure 8 The climbing areas.

The Cader Idris Group

The long whale-back of high ridges reaching to the sea to the south of Barmouth.

Best gateways: By train or car to Dolgellau, or Tal-y-Llyn.

Youth Hostels at Dolgellau, Dinas Mawddwy, Corris.

Initial Expedition

An ascent of Pen-y-Gader, 2927 feet/893 metres, by the Foxes Path, starting near Dolgellau. Return the same way or over to Tal-y-Llyn via Cwm Cau.

Longer Expedition

A traverse of the range starting from Cross Foxes. Westwards over Mynydd Moel, Pen-y-Gader and Tryau Mawr to the sea near Fairbourne Station. A twelve-mile/twenty-kilometre ridge walk followed by a swim!

The Brecon Beacons

A National Park covering miles of fine mountain country.

Best gateways: By train to Brecon.
By road north from Cardiff or Swansea or west from England and Abergavenny.

Youth Hostels at Crickhowell, Tyn-y-Cae, Llwyn-y-celyn, Capel-y-ffin, Llanddeusant.

Expeditions

From Talybont-on-Usk westwards over Bryn to the summit ridge at 2504 feet/763 metres, on to the Tor Glas col and up over Pen-y-Fan, 2907 feet/885 metres, to drop down to the Storry Arms Youth Hostel. Twelve miles/twenty kilometres.

Or up to the top of Carmarthen Van from Llanddeusant Youth Hostel, by way of the Banau Sir Gaer ridge. Returning down the north ridge over Mynydd Llan, or down Fan Hir to the Senny Bridge–Ystradgynlais road.

Dartmoor

A 1000-foot-plus/300 metres National Trust moorland area between Okehampton, Two Bridges, Tavistock and Widecombe.

Best gateways: By train to Okehampton.
By road to Two Bridges.

Youth Hostels at Bellever, Gidleigh, Steps Bridge, Tavistock.

Expeditions

Good map-reading practice anywhere in the area. The Moor is over twelve miles/twenty kilometres across and sparsely populated, so don't underrate its lack of height.

Try a crossing from north to south, over Yes Tor, High Willhays and the Black Ridge.

The Chiltern Hills

Reaching from Oxford to Dunstable.

Best gateways: Dunstable, Ivinghoe, Tring, Amersham.

Youth Hostels at Ivinghoe, Lee Gate.

Expeditions

From the Dunstable Gap west to Ashridge and Ivinghoe on National Trust property. Or west from Amersham up on to the ridge. Good walks, but watch out for private property.

The North Downs

Stretching from Guildford to Reigate at about the 600-foot/80-metre level.

Best gateways: By train to Guildford, Dorking or Reigate.
By road to Albury Down, Mickleham, or
Headley.

Youth Hostels at Tanners Hatch, Holmbury St Mary.

Expeditions

From Guildford up to the Albury Downs and along the
Ancient Trackway to Dorking. (10–12 miles/16–20 kilometres of fine walking and needing some accurate map-
reading.)

From Burford Bridge up on to Box Hill, then a grand
circuit round to Pebble Coombe, across Headley Common,
out to the Leatherhead Downs and then south to Mickleham
and back to Burford (ten miles/sixteen kilometres of heath
and minor paths through beech trees. Again take a map.)

The Sandstone Rocks of South-East England

Part of the Weald where the rock is exposed and climbable.
Harrison's Rocks – near Groombridge, Kent. These rocks
  are extremely popular and provide opportunities for practice climbing for beginners and experts. O.S. 1:50000
  Map 188. Sq. 5335.
High Rocks, near Tunbridge Wells. O.S. 1:50000 Map
  188. Sq. 5538.
Bowles Rocks, near Eridge. Courses only available to
  novices by booking.

Climbing on outcrops is almost a complete sport in itself.
The 15–35-foot/5–10-metre cliffs are usually steep, and most
climbers use a 'top-rope' technique to safeguard their upward progress. An illustrated guidebook to all the outcrops
of the south-east is available from most mountaineering
shops.

Derbyshire

The centre of England becomes high and wild to the north of Matlock, and gives walks in abundance.

Best gateways: Glossop, Edale, Hope, Millers Dale, Buxton. All by train or bus.

Youth Hostels at Matlock Bath, Shining Cliff, Buxton, Bretton, Eyam, Windgather, Edale, Hagg Farm, Youlgrave and several other places.

Expeditions

The Peak itself is not always an 'easy day for ladies', particularly in bad weather. Fine walks above Edale to Jacob's Ladder and across the moor to Kinder Downfall. Or south of Castleton to Peveril Castle and the top of the Winnats.

This area is littered with outcrops of Millstone Grit, which make excellent climbing grounds. Best-known rocks at:

Black Rocks, near Cromford. O.S. 1:50000 Map 119. Sq. 2955.

Brassington Rocks. O.S. 1:50000 Map 119. Sq. 2154.

Cratcliff Tor, near Winster. O.S. 1:50000 Map 119. Sq. 2262.

Stanage Edge, near Hathersage. O.S. 1:50000 Map 119. Sq. 2385.

Baslow, near Bakewell. O.S. 1:50000 Map 119. Sq. 2472.

Kinder, near Hayfield. O.S. 1:50000 Map 119. Sq. 0889.

(*See* Chapter 9 for Guidebooks.)

Cross Fell and Mickle Fell

The Pennine Chain from the Wharfe to the Tyne gives

thrilling walking and often far more lonely days than do the western hills.

Best gateways: Alston or Appleby by train or road.

Youth Hostels at Langdon Beck, Nine Banks, Acomb, Once Brewed.

Expeditions

Over the Milburn Forest from the Caldron Snout in the south to Cross Fell in the north.

Or walk the Roman Wall, with its twenty-mile/32-kilometre section crossing the mountains.

The Lake District

Lakes, peaks and valleys radiating from Scafell.

Best gateways: By train to Windermere or Keswick.
By road to Grasmere, Langdale, Coniston, Borrowdale or Wastwater.

Youth Hostels at Eskdale, Ambleside, Grasmere, Buttermere, Patterdale, Honister Hause, Wastwater and fourteen others.

Expeditions

This area provides some of the best walking in the world. High and narrow passes lead from one valley to another and always the views are changing. Good map-reading needed, as the 'wrong' valley can be a long way from home, food and bed!

Initial walks: From the Old Dungeon Gill Hotel at the head of Great Langdale, north-west to Rossett Gill, up to Esk Hause and from the col, either go south over Scafell Pikes (3210 feet/978 metres) and down Lingmell Gill to Wasdale Head, or north to Sty Head and the Borrowdale Valley.

From Wythburn, Thirlmere, up on to Helvellyn (3118 feet/950 metres), and then down to the north over Whiteside to Thirlspot.

More advanced routes: Traverse over Swirral and Striding Edge on Helvellyn, starting and finishing at Patterdale.

The Langdale Skyline. Over the Langdale Pikes and round the watershed to Rossett Crag, Bow Fell, Crinkle Crags and Wrynose Fell.

From Eskdale, over Scafell and down to Sty Head, up over Great Gable (2949 feet/898 metres), back to Green Gable and so along the ridge to Honister Pass.

This whole area simply asks to be explored. I suggest you finish reading this book, buy a map, and get cracking yourself. You'll find the mountain paths link up the whole area.

N.B. For a good long day, in the footsteps of the Romans, try the High Street walk, which follows the Roman road from Sockbridge in the north to Troutbeck. The road stays above the 2000-foot/600-metre contour line for nearly eight miles/thirteen kilometres and must have enjoyed quite a reputation with the legions.

Scotland

To the north of Edinburgh and Glasgow, the counties of Inverness, Banff, Aberdeen, Ross and Cromarty, and Sutherland give magnificent climbing. The island of Skye is world famous for its ridge walks.

Best gateways: By train to Fort William, Aviemore, Kyle of Lochalsh.

By road to Glencoe, Braemar.

Expeditions

The whole area provides endless scope for walking and scrambling. To those who are going to Scotland for the first time I suggest that they climb in the Fort William–Glencoe region, as this is the most famous area.

1   An ascent of Ben Nevis – follow the pony track the first time and have a good look at the mountain. Remember that many Scottish mountains start at sea-level, so a height on the map of 4406 feet/1342·5 metres for Ben Nevis means that you have exactly that much of ascent to do from Fort William.

2   In Glencoe – a traverse of the Aonach Eagach ridge which guards the north side of the pass; or to the south a visit to the Hidden Valley and Bidean nam Bian (3766 feet/ 1147·5 metres).

With more experience a trip to Skye will be good sport, while on the opposite side of Scotland the Cairngorms await your pleasure.

These dozen areas, dealt with so briefly here, are the key to your British climbing. The expeditions outlined are only for your initial guidance. When you are with other mountain-walkers keep your ears open and you will soon hear of many other fine expeditions. When you are on the high peaks keep your eyes open and you will see other ridges which will lead you to strange valleys and fresh peaks on future occasions.

4 Finding the Way

If you have ever been caught out in a thick pea-soup fog, you will know how easy it is to be lost, even within a few yards of your own front door in a street that you know like the back of your hand. On the mountains mist and cloud is never of a thick green constituency, it is white or grey. Unless it is night or snowing hard it is always possible to see fifty yards or so. But mountains have few signposts or name-plates on them, and if you wish to return home safely and on time, then you will have to learn to use and trust the map and compass.

They never give you wrong advice and are better than a 'hunch' when you are in doubt. Mountains look entirely different in mist and cloud, and, just as in a city fog, it is possible to be lost on a path that you have walked many times before. One Easter I was with a friend on Crib Goch in Wales. We had traversed from Cwm Glas round the mountain keeping about 500 feet/150 metres below the ridge. Mist swirled around us and somehow or other, in spite of our keeping a good look-out, we crossed the path that leads up the east ridge without noticing it. As we traversed scree slopes and scrambled over rotten rock, I realized that we had missed the track, and so we turned downhill to meet the Pyg Track.

After a while we came to the path, or a path, for even though I had walked the Pyg Track a hundred times during the past three years, this piece of path was strange to me.

It sloped from left down to right. My friend suggested that 'home and a hot bath' lay to the right. My map and compass said 'left'. We went left and gradually the path flattened out, and my friend was beginning to congratulate me on my map-reading, when suddenly, within several moments of each other, two parties loomed through the mist and passed us going in the opposite direction. At once common sense cast doubt on our judgement. What would two groups of climbers be doing making for the top of Snowdon in the twilight? Obviously it was we who were going up! Out came the map and compass again, and as before they confirmed our present direction. We continued for ten doubtful minutes, and then to our relief the valley of Llanberis came into view, and we were, as the map noted, on the Pyg Track.

The moral of this story is not that I was cleverer than my friend, but that the map and compass are never wrong. The conflicting evidence of the slope and the other parties would have soon led us wrongly, had we been without map and compass.

Why didn't we ask the other parties the way? Well, we didn't want to hurt our pride. You all know what follows pride – in this case it was the 'downfall' that we wanted.

The Map

Maps come in all shapes, colours and sizes. Some of them, like the ones in the back of a diary, get the whole world on one small page. Others, like town street plans, take several square feet to reproduce one square mile. The best map by far for mountain walking is the new 1:50000 Ordnance Survey Map, or where this map is still not available, our old friend the 1 inch to the mile O.S. map. These maps are the basic sources of information for mountaineers and

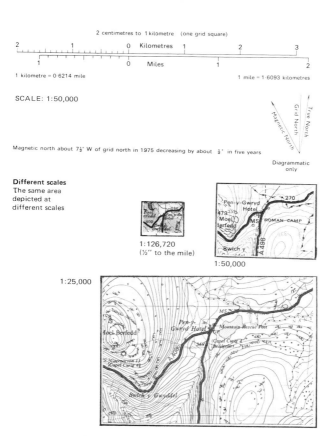

2 centimetres to 1 kilometre (one grid square)

2   1   0   Kilometres   1   2   3

1   0   Miles   1   2

1 kilometre = 0·6214 mile

1 mile = 1·6093 kilometres

SCALE: 1:50,000

Magnetic north about 7½° W of grid north in 1975 decreasing by about ½° in five years

True North

Grid North

Magnetic North

Diagrammatic
only

Different scales
The same area
depicted at
different scales

1:126,720
(½" to the mile)

1:50,000

1:25,000

Examples of the same area of ground as depicted at different
scales. Notice how the map maker has 25 times as much space
to describe the ground from the ½ inch scale to the 2½ inch scale.

ramblers in Britain. The new 1 : 50000 map has proved that the O.S. can still produce cartography as good as any other country in the world. The scale gives about $1\frac{1}{4}$ inches/2 centimetres of paper for every mile/kilometre of terrain. Plenty of space for the mapper to draw in the detail that we need for hand-rails in the hills when we use a map for navigation. With this map it is possible to walk for forty kilometres and identify every farm, stream and mountain during the day.

The Bartholomew's 'Half-Inch' map, although excellent for cycling, does not give enough detail for walking, while the large scale 1 : 25000 map is rather too detailed for normal navigation, but where real accuracy is wanted this $2\frac{1}{2}$ inches to the mile map is essential, for it includes walls and other boundaries in its detail. For in really horrible weather walls and fences become the only really certain clues when the path is lost.

All 1 : 50000 and 1-inch O.S. maps have a grid frame of squares superimposed on them. The side of this square is 1000 metres long, and for most practical purposes the vertical lines are True North.

Map References

These lines are used for pin-pointing places accurately. Six-figure references that are correct to about 100 metres can give the position of a camp-site or rendezvous. This method is very useful, for often a verbal description of a place is long and even then ambiguous.

To find a six-figure reference this is the way:

(*See* map on page 54.)

Example

Summit Station on Snowdon

East		*North*	
Take west edge of grid square in which point lies and read the figure printed opposite this line on the north or south margins	60	Take south edge of grid square in which point lies and read the figures printed opposite this line on the east and west margins	54
Estimate tenths eastwards	9	Estimate tenths northwards	4
	609		544
Full map reference is 609544			

Using the same technique the reference for the Pen-y-Pass Youth Hostel is 647557 – and 642547 you will find is not a good camp-site!

The most frequent mistake made in working out map-references is to quote the wrong three figures first; on many maps a quick check would find what was wrong, but on some maps the figures at the sides are similar to the ones at the top and bottom. Consequently it would be possible to be completely in the wrong place with one of these 'inverted' bearings. I find the following dodge keeps me right.

Pretend that the bottom edge of the map is a street with the house numbers along it. The houses are tall blocks of flats, with the numbers marked in the side margins of the map. Now I say to myself, if I wish to visit a friend who lives in this area, the first thing I do is to find the right block – so I go and check the numbers at the bottom of the map first.

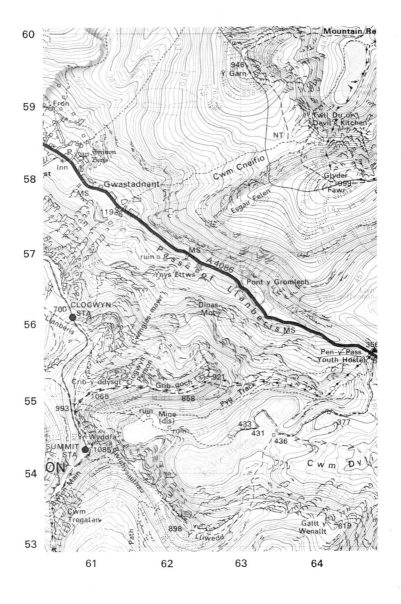

Only when I have done this do I worry about which floor the flat is on – and I check the side numbers for this.

You'll find this makes it very simple – remember – 'always go along the street first before going upstairs'.

Setting the Map

On the top of Box Hill, and on the top of many other high points, there is a sort of table which has a map engraved on it. This map is simple to use – you just stand behind it, pick out a named point on the table and look up in the same direction; there you will find, directly beyond, the actual place on the ground. This table is what we call 'set' or 'orientated'.

A map can be used the same way with accuracy when it is 'set', that is held so that north on the map points to north on the ground. When this has been done a line drawn from your position on the map to an object should, if continued, pass through the actual place on the ground.

Even without a compass it is easy to set a map, especially when you are on top of a known peak. Put the map down on a flat surface and twist it round until a line drawn from the peak you are on to another known object is in the same direction on map and ground. When this is done then all the surrounding valleys, peaks and passes are easy to identify. (*See* Fig. 9.)

With a compass it is possible to set the map by just twisting it round until it is in a north position. Just place the compass on a N–S grid line and then twist the map around until the needle points to the top of the map. The map is now fairly accurately set. (*See* Fig. 10.)

Opposite: Snowdon. (1:50 000 scale).

Figure 9A Compare map with landscape: church on wrong side of river, high peak's ridge on wrong side of mountain etc. Map is obviously not 'set'.

Conventional Signs and Contours

In between the grey-blue grid lines is a mass of information about the country that the map represents. By being able to understand the map-makers' language it is possible to read a map like a book. The 'alphabet' or 'code' is all contained

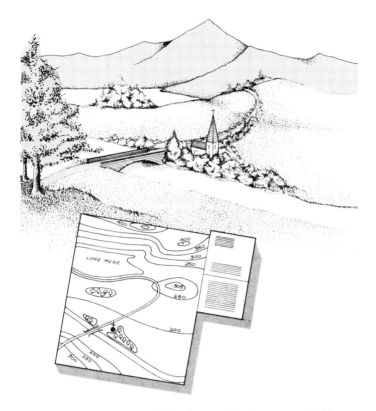

Figure 9B Compare map with landscape: church on correct side of river, road bends the correct way across hill etc. Map fits landscape, is 'set'.

in the margin of the one-inch map. It is called – Conventional Signs. Luckily most of these signs are small drawings and hence self-explanatory. With a reasonable memory, a couple of hours' study will enable most people to learn-off the language of the map.

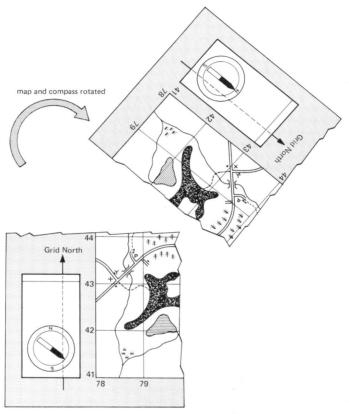

Figure 10 Setting the map by compass.

When abroad it will be necessary to study a new language as foreign maps use different symbols to our own.

In mountainous parts of the country, in which we are particularly interested, brown squiggly lines dominate the map. These are the very important, to the mountaineer, 'contour-lines'. These lines indicate the rise and fall of the ground and mark off the fifty-foot vertical intervals on the 1:50000 maps. (*See* Fig. 11.) Now and again 'spot-heights', marked thus – .433, fill in the picture of the surface of the land. Spot-heights have been surveyed accurately, while points marked like this – △ 1065, are Trigonometrical stations and their heights have been determined with the greatest accuracy as the basis of the original survey of the country. On 1:50000 scale maps the spot-heights are given in metres. On many summits you will find a concrete obelisk about three or four feet high marking a 'Trig-point'.

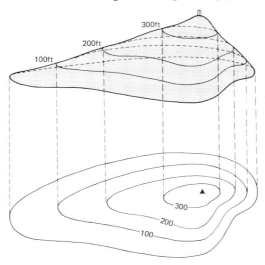

Figure 11 Contours.

A practised mountaineer can 'see' an area in his mind's-eye by just looking at the contours on a map. The shape of the valleys, the steepness of the slopes, the height of cliffs are all made crystal-clear by contour-lines.

59

When the contours are crammed close together then steep slopes are expected, slopes (whether they be convex or concave) can be worked out by a little observation. (*See* Fig. 12.) Valleys are easy to pick out, in any case they usually have rivers or streams in them, by looking for the upward pointing V of the contours. It is easy to remember which way the contours point in a valley by noting that at the coast a river comes out of a V-shaped estuary and that the contours follow this pattern right back up to the hills.

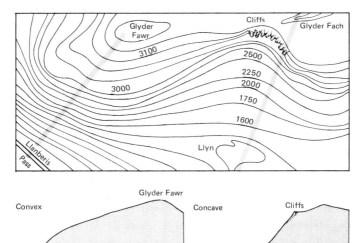

Figure 12 Types of slope.

If is often necessary, and always interesting, to know if a certain place can be seen from another in the mountains. The map gives the answer to this problem, too. First lay a piece of paper on the map and join up the two points, then mark off on the paper each contour as it crosses the edge (Fig. 13). Next make a vertical scale on the piece of paper

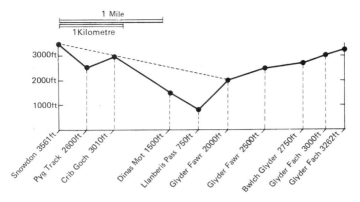

Figure 13 Intervisibility. A line from Snowdon to Glyder Fach is unbroken, so it is possible to see one summit from the other. Snowdon will be hidden by Crib Goch until a height of 2200 feet/670 metres is reached on Glyder Fawr – see dotted line.

and project lines up from the contour marks to the appropriate height. Join up these marks and you will have a section of the area. Now if a straight line from one point to the other is not cut by the section – then intervisibility is possible. Remember when making a section that a rise in the ground with a fair amount of area above its last contour will probably be thirty to forty feet/nine to twelve metres higher than that last contour ring. Hills seldom have flat and level tops.

The Compass

Most people who walk and climb in the hills of this country carry a compass of some sort or other. Heavy ex-army survey instruments are carried by some, while others tuck in their pocket the kind of compass that comes on the end of a key-ring. All of them feel safer for having a compass

61

with them, and they attach some magical property to the small piece of magnetized needle. Few of them really know how to use the compass properly. It may seem to be miraculous that this magnetized needle always points in the same direction, but the compass will give far more protection if it is used as a scientific instrument, and not as the mountaineer's equivalent of a St Christopher's charm.

A compass is an essential piece of mountaineering equipment, and it can save your life – or, more mundanely, get you home in time for tea – only if you can use it.

The most accurate compass is the prismatic sighting type used by surveyors and built to a high standard. But in spite of its undoubted hairline accuracy the prismatic is not the best compass for mountain work. As it costs over £30, perhaps it is just as well that this is so. Its disadvantages, besides expense, are heaviness, vulnerability and awkwardness when used as a protractor.

Streets ahead in everything except accuracy to half a degree is the new type compass mounted on a plastic protractor base. These compasses have revolutionized map and compass work for the mountaineer.

The best known make is the Silva, manufactured in Sweden by the family that invented the system of combining a compass needle with a protractor. They market about a dozen models but there are several that are especially useful for mountaineers. The Type 7 is the best for the young and impecunious climber – it will provide exactness and has the same high quality needle and capsule that the more expensive models use. Price about £3.

The Type 3 is slightly larger and boasts a magnifying glass and luminous spots; this model costs around £4. The best compass for the experienced mountaineer is the Type 4. This compass has romer scales for checking six-figure grid references and is big enough to be used for long bearings – cost about £6·50.

The Silva Compass Type 4 has romer scales for 1:25000,
1:50000 (the new O.S. scale) and 1:63360 (1 inch to 1 mile) –
essential for calculating six-figure references accurately.
Liquid-filled anti-static housing; precision sapphire bearings and
Swedish steel needle; shatterproof base-plate with magnifier lens;
luminous points and graduated scales in inches and millimetres.

You will expect your compass to do two jobs – first to
give a direction with a needle that is accurate, quick to
settle and easy to read by night as well as day. Secondly, to
give good results when used as a protractor, so that vital
bearings can be found quickly from the map.

Compass Bearings

Many mountaineers spend some time before an outing on
the hills, especially in bad weather, in compiling a set of
compass bearings for the day's walk. I have a friend who can
quote some of the more important bearings off by heart.
For instance, he can tell you at once on what bearing you
must walk when leaving the top of Glyder Fawr to reach
the difficult-to-find-in-cloud Devil's Kitchen Path – 339
degrees magnetic is his answer if you wish to check it. (This
ground is covered by the map on page 54; Glyder Fawr is
at 643579 and the path-top is at 638587.)

You don't have to be the Astronomer Royal, or even a good mathematician, to understand bearings. There is nothing complicated about them as long as you remember a few basic principles.

A bearing is just another name for the number of degrees in the angle between your intended line of direction and north. (*See* Fig. 14.) And here comes the biggest complication – what north? Do I mean true north – which is the North Pole; or grid north – which is parallel to the vertical edge of a survey map; or magnetic north – which is the direction that the compass needle points?

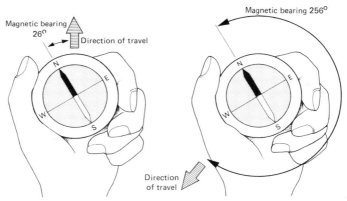

Figure 14 Magnetic bearings.

Only if you lived in certain parts of the United States or Canada would you find that magnetic and true north were identical. Lucky Chicago. For most practical purposes in this country we usually regard true and grid north as being the same, although this is not strictly true. But we do have to make allowances for the big, nearly eight degrees, disparity between magnetic and grid bearings. (*See* Fig. 15.)

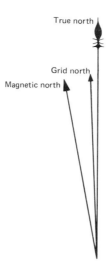

Figure 15 The three norths.

In the margin of all Ordnance Survey Maps you will find this difference explained. At the moment in 1977, magnetic north is about seven and a half degrees west of grid north for most of the country. This declination is decreasing by about half a degree every eight years, so by about the year 2095 we shall have nothing to worry about, except that then the error will gradually build up again in the opposite direction.

Take a bearing – first from the map. Draw a thin pencil line joining together the two places that you are interested in. (*See* Fig. 16.) Then with a protractor measure the angle between this line and the vertical grid lines. This angle is your bearing – but remember it is a grid bearing. If you wish to use this bearing on the actual ground, then you must convert to a magnetic one by adding on seven and a half degrees.

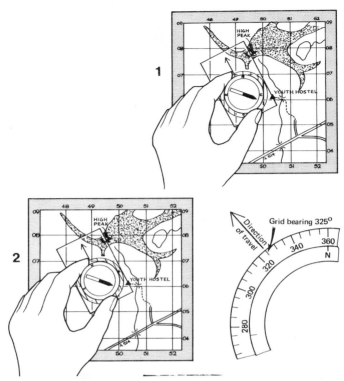

Figure 16 The Silva system.
1. Place the long edge of the compass so that it joins up the
starting point with the destination (Youth Hostel and High Peak).
Ignore the compass needle.
2. Now turn the compass dial until 'N' on the rim points to the
top of the map. Use the grid lines for total accuracy. The figure
opposite the direction of travel arrow is the grid bearing – 325°.

Reversing this procedure and using the compass first we
can take a bearing on the ground. Stand holding your
compass and turn round until the needle points to north on
the rim of the compass. Now the angle between this needle
and a line crossing over the compass from your object is

66

your magnetic bearing. (*See* Fig. 14.) To convert this to a grid bearing for identification on a map it will be necessary to subtract seven and a half degrees.

The most common mistake that people make when converting bearings is to sometimes add when they should subtract and vice versa. To cure this fault try and learn this little mnemonic:

*M*agnetic to *G*rid – *S*ubtract; *G*rid to *M*agnetic – *A*dd.
Men Generally Say – Great Minds Agree.

Use the initial letters to keep things the right way round.

When using a compass to take a bearing be careful that you are getting a proper reading. Army manuals warn us of 'concealed errors', for instance, a heavy artillery unit will affect the compass needle up to sixty yards/fifty metres away. You will be unfortunate if you come across a couple of howitzers during a day on the hills, but you may well be troubled by other smaller, and often forgotten influences. The pouch pocket of the anorak is often the obvious place to keep a strong knife, and as it will only be a few inches away from the compass when you are using it, some error will result. If you want accurate readings check on metal near the compass before taking a bearing.

When I was organizing a compass race on the South Downs I was mystified as to why one leg of the course gave so much trouble. After watching several students 'set' their course on this section, I saw the answer. Most of them were placing their compass to get it steady on top of a fence post, around which was wrapped several feet of barbed wire. The needle was being swung about fifteen degrees by this disturbance. Magnetic mountains and underground veins of iron stone that affect compasses are fairly few and far between, although it is generally agreed that there are spots on the Main Cuillin Ridge in Skye where the compass needle is unfaithful for once to its home in the Viscount Melville Sound.

The Silva compass short circuits the bearing taking procedure, and hence avoids many of the pitfalls that novices and experts occasionally fall into.

The Silva System can be as simple as 1, 2, 3. In Fig. 16 stages 1 and 2 – finding a bearing from a map – are explained. Fig. 17 shows stage 3 – seeing where the bearing points. The only snag to this simple routine is magnetic deviation, which means that we have to take note of the eight degrees difference between our grid and magnetic norths.

Figure 17 Stage 3 of the Silva system. Turn the compass until the red end of the needle points to 'N' on the dial rim. Your destination is now pointed out by the direction of travel arrow.

An excellent way of doing this and keeping the 1, 2, 3 Silva System intact is to stick a small piece of white tape on the underside of the compass from the centre of the dial up to 352 degrees on the rim. Now instead of turning around in Stage 3 until the needle points to north on the dial of the compass, you just rotate a little further until it points to 352 degrees and lines up with your guide-line sticker. (*See* Fig. 18.)

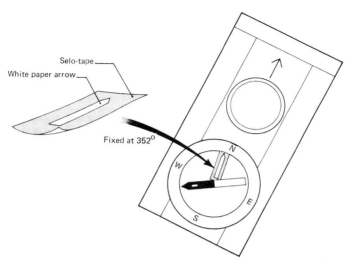

Figure 18 In stage 3 of the Silva system any correction for
magnetic variation can be avoided if the compass needle is
aligned on 352° and not to 'N' (assuming that the magnetic
variation is 8° west). A slip of white paper stuck on the base of
the capsule with sellotape helps to locate the exact mark.

When you are adept at taking bearings and finding that
the results tally when converted for use on the ground or
map, you will be capable of using them to find your way in
bad weather or at night. With the correct bearing noted on
your compass and the needle pointing to north on the rim,
look up at your line of direction and pick out a rock or tree
or something distinctive that lies on your path, put the
compass away and walk to this place. Then with your back
to this object repeat the procedure. In this way you are
walking on a bearing.

In snow or mist, when natural markers are difficult to
pick out, your climbing partner will have to substitute. He
walks ahead of you keeping in the right direction by your

shouts – 'Left a bit', or 'Move over to the right'. When he has nearly disappeared tell him to stand still, you then rejoin him and the pattern is repeated. Much to my surprise I once found my way in thick driving snow from the Llyn y Cwn, at the top of the Devil's Kitchen, to Llyn Cwm-y-ffynnon, above Pen-y-Gwryd in North Wales, by this method. I was with a party of schoolboys from Anglesey and we were all heavily laden with camping gear. We could barely see more than the length of a cricket pitch. We kept moving slowly and from the end of the group I checked every few yards on my compass and by shouts kept the front man on the right line. This method was reasonably accurate because we were moving very slowly, if we had been moving more quickly I would have had more difficulty in checking deviations before they became pronounced.

In patchy weather, when windows of views open and shut around you at irregular intervals, it is possible to use a couple of bearings to fix your position. That is as long as you can recognize some of the things that you glimpse.

One winter Chris Brasher and I were making a circuit of the skyline at the head of Great Langdale, in the Lake District. We had done a climb on Bowfell Buttress on the way round and it was now misty and growing dark as we continued the traverse. The question was – on which part of the ridge were we?

We had already disagreed once on our estimated position but had been put right – both of us – by finding the Three Tarns. Now we were beginning to wonder if we had missed the col above Red Tarn and were on the south side of Pike of Blisco, or if our speed was less than we hoped and that we were still traversing Cold Pike. Just as we were settling for pressing on along the water-shed, a brief clearing to our left gave us a quick look at what we recognized as Gimmer Crag. Almost before we had noted a bearing on this cliff the gap in the cloud closed and opened again seconds later showing us the white walls of the Old Dungeon Ghyll Hotel down in Langdale. Our first reading on Gimmer was forty-eight degrees, and the second one on the hotel was seventy-three degrees. We converted these figures to grid bearings and projected them back on to the map. Where the two lines crossed was our position. To our dismay we found that we were still on the side of Crinkle Crags, at least a mile and a half/2·5 kilometres from where we had hoped. (*See* Fig. 19.)

We cut our losses and descended down Oxendale, reaching the road with just enough light to pick out our footsteps. Had we pressed on thinking that we were near the end of the skyline we would have been benighted somewhere on the side of Black Wars, and would have spent an uncomfortable few hours finding our way down rocky Brown Gill in the pitch dark.

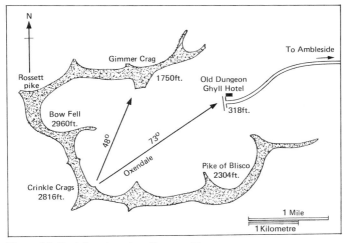

Figure 19 Back bearings locating position.

Direction Without a Compass or Map

Although a compass can't be beaten, because it works round the clock under any conditions, we can, by keeping our eyes open, dispense with its use, except in particularly difficult places.

This wayfinding by natural signs, using the stars and the sun, is still a valuable art in many parts of the world. Primitive tribes and nomads rely, for the most part, on anything but the compass. On clear sky days the sun and the stars will give us direction with accuracy.

By the Sun

The apparent traverse of the sun round the earth is clockwise in the Northern hemisphere and with the aid of a watch it is possible to find north.

First, point the hour hand at the sun. Then the line that bisects the angle between the figure twelve and the hour hand points to the south. (*See* Fig. 20.) Always remember that it will be necessary to take an hour off during British summer time.

By the Stars

The Pole Star is never more than two and a quarter degrees from due north; in fact twice during the twenty-four hours it is exactly north. This 'mariner's star' is easy to find, if you can recognize the Great Bear or Plough group of stars. The pointers of the Plough give the game away all the time. (*See* Fig. 21.)

With the establishment of north it is easy to work out the other points of the compass. For finding more exact degrees, work out your own scale or 'rule of thumb'. Stand with your

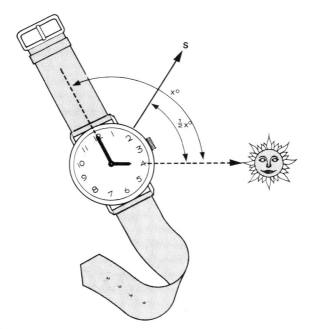

Figure 20 Direction by watch and sun.

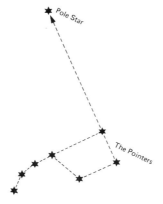

Figure 21 The Plough.

right hand stretched out in front of you with the fingers and thumb spread out. Mark a starting point on the horizon and see how many spans take you right round the skyline and back to the starting point. Mine comes to twenty, which means that my span subtends an angle of 360 degrees divided by 20 – which is 18 degrees.

Many other small clues can help to work out direction. In our British climbing areas, the prevailing wind which blows most of the year comes from the west. Even when the wind is not blowing you will see around you the effect it has had. Trees, bushes and even clumps of grass will often be bent and shaped away from the wind and towards the east. Branches will be longer on the sheltered side. Moss, which prefers shade and damp, will be usually found on the north side of tree trunks and walls. (Fig. 22.)

At night-time when the stars are obscured it will still be possible to see the light in the sky to the west, even several hours after sunset. Before dawn if you are still out, the sky in the east will be less dark than elsewhere.

Figure 22 Direction signs – wind-blown tree and mossy wall.

Direction finding is all part of the game of mountaineering and it is never necessary to be lost if the above rules are followed. Remember that the early Phoenicians and Vikings found their way halfway round the world with the same 'clues' that you have to use today, and with much inferior compasses and maps.

5 The Best Way Up

Many years ago when I was first finding my way round the local hills, I set out from the small village of Aberllefenni – where family holidays were spent – to climb to a ridge called Maes-y-glase. The ridge dominated the northern skyline and was about four miles/six kilometres away. Family Sunday-afternoon walks and bilberry picking expeditions had not reached the ridge by half, and I was anxious to see what there was to see over the other side.

As I stormed out of the village, keeping to the narrow-gauge railway that served the slate-quarry, I caught up with a local shepherd and his dog. He was off to walk his mountain 'run' in order to check his flock. I quickly passed him, for I had a long way to go and had no time for gossip. The 'tram-way' as the railway is called contoured round the hillside. This was no good to me and soon I struck out straight for the ridge in front of me. I made for the skyline and worked hard for the next couple of hours. As I wearily climbed the last few feet to the summit of Maen Du, a dog ran down to meet me. It looked suspiciously like the dog I had passed earlier in the day. When I found the farmer sitting at the foot of a cairn I knew it was!

'Have a good walk?' he enquired.

There he sat, he was cool – I was hot, he was still clean and tidy – I was scratched and dirty, he was still dry-footed – my feet and stockings were soaked. Obviously, although our destination was the same our paths had been somewhat

Mist can turn a familiar walk into a serious expedition where a wrong choice of route along a ridge can involve a party in long delays.

different. In fact he had used a path, while I had used nothing – neither path nor common sense.

Most paths in wild country have been made by professionals – farmers, drovers, quarry-men, miners and guides have all contributed to the worn tracks across rock and grass. Some of the more popular ones are now roads that join two valleys together. Men who make the same journey every day throughout the year will pick out the most economical route. They take into consideration everything that makes the path less fatiguing. Mountain trails are seldom straight for long; even the Romans, the stoutest supporters of the straight line, knew that in mountains it wasn't always the quickest way between two points. On the other hand, quickness was a desirable quality and the early path-makers would only make a detour for a very good reason. Every bend was due to a particular piece of local knowledge. These factors are not always apparent to the novice in the mountains, and he will do well to remember that a good path will do the following:

1 Gain height gradually but surely.
2 Avoid wet ground and bogs.
3 Keep to firm ground, keeping clear of loose scree and deep heather.
4 Avoid steep rocks and gullies.
5 Keep to the leeward of ridges.
6 Be well marked with cairns.

Most of our British hills have at least one good path to the summit, but it would be very dull if we were always expected to keep to the track. Mountaineers get a great deal of fun and satisfaction out of creating their own ways, but such ways if they are to be good must be based on the six rules set out above.

If you serve a fair apprenticeship on ready-made paths you will soon begin to understand them. You will develop a 'feel' for mountain country, and an 'eye' for a good route. The path will begin to do what you expect it to do and you will be able to predict the layout of a path without previous knowledge. When you have reached this happy stage, you will be all set to make your own way whenever you wish.

With experience you can correlate the natural features of the land at a glance, picking out the likely snags to progress several miles ahead. Bogs and marsh have their own particular vegetation – lush green moss and tall grasses. Heather and bracken, for all their inconvenience, seldom grow on damp ground. Cliffs usually form screes beneath them, but sheep tracks usually cross such screes at the foot of the cliff. Spurs are always well drained and usually give good gradients and access to the peaks. Stream beds are poor

Figure 23 Cairn.

paths, winding and littered with boulders. Slopes look less steep from below and more steep from above, than they really are. These and a dozen other observations will help the experienced climber to arrive safely and economically at his journey's end.

Speed in the Mountains

If you are making mountain journeys, it is always necessary to have a fairly reasonable idea of your time of arrival. It might be to catch a train or bus at the end of a week-end, or to be on the doorstep of a hostel at opening-time. It is very easy to under-estimate the time needed to cross hilly and difficult country.

Before starting in the morning it is possible to work out the length of your proposed route by stretching a piece of cotton across the map – this will tell you how many miles it is on the 'flat'. Here, of course, is the snag – there seldom is any 'flat'.

Most people find that when walking along an open road they can average about 4 m.p.h./6·5 k.p.h. and still enjoy life. If they were to move over on to the rough grass verge, they would find that their speed was reduced to 3 m.p.h./5 k.p.h. for the same effort involved.

In the mountains you will not only have to cope with rough going under foot, but gravity as well. To help you estimate your speed in such country the following formula called 'Naismith's Rule' is very useful:

'Allow an hour for every three miles/five kilometres as measured on the map, and an hour for every 1500 feet/450 metres climbed.'

Therefore if your mountain top is six miles/ten kilometres away and 3000 feet/900 metres above the starting point, the outward journey will take four hours and the return journey two hours making a total of six hours. (*See* Fig. 24.) Naturally, if you enjoy long rests, and diversions for rock scrambling *en route*, it will be necessary to add some time to this formula. In any case after a little experience you will be able to compile your own personal formula which will take into consideration your own special idiosyncrasies. Walking with a heavy pack will also mean adaptation of the formula to match your fitness.

The Special Needs of the Mountain Walking Party

First and foremost make sure that it is a party. Solitary climbing is extremely dangerous especially to the novice or

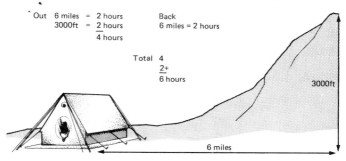

Figure 24 Naismith's rule.

even to the experienced in a strange group of mountains. On your own, even an otherwise trivial twisted ankle could lead to benightment and the consequent possibility of exposure.

Three or four together makes a good party – not too large to become spread-out over several miles, and not too small to prevent one member going for help if it is wanted.

When the party starts out at the beginning of the day it is an excellent idea to leave a message with someone. Just a brief note stating the day's programme. Many Youth Hostels have special log books in which it is possible to enter the names of the members of the party and their destination and expected time of arrival, together with the proposed route. A note pinned to a sleeping-bag inside a tent will serve the same purpose if difficulties arise. The British mountains although relatively small can be quite big enough to lose a walker incapacitated by a damaged leg. Many a search-party has failed to find a victim of such an accident simply because it had no clue as to which way to concentrate its search. It is not every day, thank goodness, that a rag-covered skeleton is found on British mountains – but it has happened!

Before leaving the valley a mountaineer should make sure that he has the following items of equipment in his sack:

Lunch Sandwiches are usually the staple lunch-time diet. Meat, tomatoes – for moisture, marmalade – it doesn't dry up like jam and honey, all make good fillings. Dates – the squashed kind, oranges and chocolate or Kendal Mint Cake will complete a fine meal. Remember that you will have to carry this food – so go for quality and not bulk. For drink – any mountain stream, as long as it is flowing fast and above human habitation, will give the finest drink in the world when you are thirsty. Don't try and drink the mountain dry.

81

The water will always be icy cold, while your inside will be very hot. Too much cold water will tend to give you severe cramp in the stomach. On long dry climbs a plastic water-bottle full of a dilute glucose and salt drink is a real bonus.

Spare Sweater A long-sleeved wool garment will keep out the cold after the sun has gone down, especially if you are still on the high ridges and moving slowly. A cagoule or water-proof cape is a must, too.

Emergency Rations In case the day goes into night, glucose will give energy just when needed and salt tablets will prevent cramp.

Simple First Aid Kit A crêpe bandage and some elastoplast should be carried. A blister can soon cut short a day if it cannot be covered as soon as it is first noticed.

Map The correct Ordnance Survey for that region. A poly-thene sandwich bag makes a very functional case for the map.

Compass A Silva protractor model. (*See* Chapter 4.)

Whistle Helpful to attract attention and guide rescue parties to the scene of the accident. The Alpine distress signal given by whistle, lamp, voice or flag consists of six blasts followed by a minute's silence and then repeated. The acknowledgement or O.K. signal, consists of three blasts followed by a minute's pause and then repeated.

Torch. Makes a long day a little shorter and safer, should the last few feet of descent be done in the dark.

6 Off the Beaten Track

Most paths in the mountains are designed for comfort –
perhaps not the walking comfort of a main road, but never-
theless they always take the line of least resistance. To the
mountaineer this is often a handicap, for although a path
may be out of the wind when it is several yards below a
ridge, it is also out of the view. For whereas the climber is
there to 'see what there is to see', the professional path user
is only interested in reaching his destination as quickly and
as easily as possible.

Consequently mountaineers are not so logical in their
choice of route. The steep way up an exposed ridge or
across rocky buttresses often attracts more than the beaten
track. Normal walking technique as described in Chapter 2
will usually suffice for paths up most British mountains, but
when you step off the path on to steeper slopes then a few
new techniques are best learnt.

Most slopes are under fifty degrees, unless they are com-
posed of rock. Grass will grow on slopes of this angle, and
can be difficult to negotiate in wet weather. Scree – made up
of small pieces of rock and usually found beneath a large
cliff, will not rest on an incline of more than about forty-five
degrees, and with care is climbable.

Unless you are competing in a fell-race or want to feel
what it is like to be on the verge of collapse, it is better to
ignore straight lines up steep slopes. Any slope over forty
degrees will be best tackled by 'tacking' – that is zig-zagging

backwards and forwards across the slope. This is rather similar to the way that a sailing-boat makes headway against the wind. If you have a bicycle you have probably used the same technique to master a hill on a quiet road. The gradient of your path will depend on the angle of your 'tack'. The more sideways you make your angle of attack, the less the gradient will be. You should try to adjust your line of attack to your own fitness. A good way of judging an economical pace uphill is to whistle or sing a tune softly. As long as you have enough surplus puff to keep making a noise, then you will not be completely creased before you reach the top.

On steep ground keep your body weight well forward and try and keep the whole foot on the ground. This position of the foot will give you a good grip with all the cleats of the boot. A tip-toe style will soon tire out the calf muscles as well as encouraging slips.

Strangely enough, at least at first sight, many climbers find that downhill work is far more tiring than going up. This is because the long descents usually come at the end of the day when leg and ankle muscles are beginning to feel the strain. It is the knee that seems to suffer most – the constant jarring of letting the body weight down on to the foot begins to make this 'shock-absorber' sore. Novices who are tired tend to make things worse by checking themselves at every stride; this increases the jarring enormously and is unnecessary. It is much better to allow the body to move a little faster and cut out the stride-by-stride jerks. Let the feet 'run on'; small quick strides will bring you to the valley much more smoothly, faster and with less effort. Naturally speed without control is dangerous, but with practice it is possible to jog down steep slopes safely and quickly, making turns every few yards to steady the pace. As in uphill work you must always keep leaning forward when descending, the tendency is to fall back and forward-lean will stop this from happening.

Some of the fastest descents are made down scree slopes and many mountains have been famous for their screes. Unfortunately, due to popularity, many of these slopes have now ceased to exist, as the small stones that covered the slope have been swept away, leaving bare rock and earth. Off the beaten track you will still find good scree slopes and with practice and agility extremely fast runs can be made. The surface, which is best made up of pieces of rock the size of tennis balls, moves under foot as you step on it.

To scree-run, first make sure that the slope is clear of small rock-faces and that it ends in a grass or heather run-out. Then start running with a shambling stride, leaning well forward and digging the heels well into the scree at each landing. It is possible to stop by making a two-footed jump, giving at the knees, letting the scree carry you a few feet until it loses its momentum. A fair amount of skill is needed to be really fast at this game, but don't worry too much if you never get to the stage when you give a joyous shout and leap down the slope like an attacking Red Indian. After watching your friends disappear, follow down at your own speed – you will soon overtake them again, they will be sitting down at the end of the scree busy emptying stones from their boots.

Good downhill scree makes very bad going in the opposite direction. With good route-finding it should never be necessary to flog up loose scree, for it is as strength sapping as trying to run up a descending escalator. At the worst it should only be essential to traverse scree. The party should always arrange itself so that one member does not roll rocks down on to another. This will mean an Indian file when crossing scree and line abreast when descending or climbing.

Sometimes it is impossible to avoid rock scree. In gullies,

for example, where it is also impossible to walk in line abreast, the party should stay as near together as possible. In this way should rocks be accidentally dislodged they will not have had time to gain dangerous momentum before they pass the last man.

A great shout of 'Below' is the accepted way of indicating that part of the mountain is adrift from its parent body, this will give those below a few seconds to leap for cover or dodge out of the way. Such a hazard for the 'tail-end Charlies' should occur seldom, for it is usually only carelessness that dislodges rocks. A good mountaineer seems to walk without moving a pebble and gets through the day without ever having to shout out a warning.

Rock-scrambling

The bare bones of a mountain stick out through the grass, heather and scree to make ridges, cliffs and pinnacles. It is on these steep rocks that climbers equipped with ropes thread their way upwards. In parties of two or three they stand on small ledges, belayed to the rock, safeguarding each other, while pulling up on small holds.

Rock-climbing is a subject for a book in itself, and in the Book List at the end of this book there is a section on such writings. In this chapter the basic principles of rock-climbing are explained in relation to rock-scrambling.

Most mountain walkers sooner or later have a go at proper rock-climbing. They get a friend to take them out on the end of a rope and they find themselves high above the paths climbing and sometimes dangling on the rope. If they have done some scrambling before they will find that they have already most of the required technique – the only difference will be the constant steepness of the rock and the consequent exposure. Most of the strenuous walks have

The Crib Goch ridge gives some of the finest scrambling in Britain, where a head for heights, good balance and precise footwork are essential.

some difficult scrambling in them, where the severity of the move-up is as hard as many moves on a proper rock-climb. The difference is that whereas on the walk the severe move is made with only a couple of feet of exposure, the same move is made on the cliff with several hundred feet of space between it and the ground below.

Before tackling such routes as the Snowdon Horseshoe, the North Ridge of Tryfan, the Aonach Eagach in Glencoe or parts of the Cuillin Ridge in Skye, it is advisable to practise rock-scrambling. This technique can be learnt on odd boulders at the side of most paths. A ten-foot/three-metre face or slab will be enough to get the feel of standing upright on rock. Pick out the footholds carefully and see what it is possible to stand on in balance without sliding back to the ground.

The most important principle is to stand upright, keeping the weight of the body right over the feet. This will help to press the boot toes down into the hold and prevent them slipping off.

'Stand upright!' and 'Get away from the rock!' are the two most commonly heard shouted instructions to beginners in rock-climbing. They apply equally well to scrambling.

Although it might seem safer to be pressed to the rock, with as much of your body touching it as possible, it is really much more insecure than standing upright. When the body is hugging the rock, the feet are pushed out and off the hold, and it is impossible to see where the next ledge is positioned. All you can see with your nose pressed against the rock is a small area about two feet/half a metre across. (*See* Fig. 25.)

Figure 25 How not to climb.

Figure 26 Good climbing position: heels down, body well away from the rock, hands low, watching feet.

When the body is upright over the legs it will mean that the weight of the body is taken by the legs, which are by far the strongest part of the human frame. It is the legs that must do the majority of the lifting of the body. A very strong gymnast might manage to pull himself up with his arms for perhaps 100 feet/30 metres, but he would be fit for nothing after that one effort. If, on the other hand, he had used his legs wherever possible and reserved his arms for special occasions, then he would have been able to continue for most of the day.

A good climber walks up his climb. (*See* Fig. 26.)

The following instructions are given to the Marines when they take a course in cliff-climbing. They apply equally well to scrambling on mountains.

1 *Stand upright*   For the reasons already given, this is *the* fundamental principle of climbing.

2 *Heels down*   This puts the boot toe in the best position to grip the rock, and helps to keep the body upright.

3 *Watch your feet*   Make sure that the foot goes straight on to the hold and doesn't just miss the right place. Once the foot has been put on the hold it should not be necessary to shuffle or adjust it at all.

4 *Hands low*   Over-reaching will pull the body into a bad position. Wherever possible use holds about head height.

5 *Test each hold*   Make sure that every piece of rock you touch or pull on is solid. Never grab at a hold, always feel it carefully first. If a hold is loose, leave it in place or lift it on to a safe ledge and warn the other members of the party of its presence.

6 *Three-point climbing*   Especially important in scrambling where no rope is used, only move one limb at a time. When you are stepping up on to a new foothold make sure that the hands are able if necessary to take all the weight should

the foot miss the grip. The same applies when the hand is searching for the best combination of holds: make sure that the feet are on good ledges.

7 *Move rhythmically* Make all movements smooth and unhurried. Jerky steps will make balance difficult. On easy rock, with experience, it is possible to work out the moves ahead and keep moving up the cliff without pause. To help steady movement avoid too high steps, always use the small intermediate foothold and break up the big strides which require such effort from the upper leg muscles.

8 *Think first* Always consider each move before it is made. An irreversible move which leads into a dead-end can soon land a climber in trouble. This can quite easily happen when scrambling down a ridge, for although it may be quite safe to let go of a ledge and drop down two or three feet to the next, it may prove impossible to regain height. Many sheep and a few climbers are rescued each year under similar circumstances.

Easy rock-climbing on a fine day is one of the best parts of mountaineering, and with some skill and a good head for heights everyone can enjoy its flavour. But remember scrambling without a rope is only justifiable on easy rock with little exposure beneath. Sheer rock-faces and slabs are strictly the preserve of roped climbers.

For obvious reasons rock-climbing is not suited to a 'trial and error' form of learning. If after several seasons of mountain-walking you are keen to attempt roped climbing try and strike up a friendship with a climber. Ask him to take you out and let you see if you like the sport. Most

Opposite. Top-rope climbing on the 40-foot (13-metre) sandstone cliffs at Bowles Rocks in Kent. Thousands of climbers from London and south-east England practise their techniques on rocks like these every week-end.

Outcrop climbing is inevitably steep and energetic and so it develops strong fingers and decisive movements.

climbers are delighted to show novices 'the ropes' and are keen to encourage new blood to the game. If you fail to find a helping hand, then there are several excellent organizations which run rock-climbing courses especially designed for the beginner. Details of such courses will be found in the last chapter of this book.

7 Winter Climbing

The climber who packs away his gear neatly in a storeroom at the end of the summer season is in danger of missing some of the finest weeks of the year on British hills.

It is the winds from the Continent that bring the snow and cold conditions. At its best a couple of days of snow is followed by a couple of weeks of clear skies, bringing sunny days and frosty nights. Such a covering of snow on the tops and ice in the streams give the mountains another complexion altogether from the summer look.

With luck, mountaineer's luck that is, a couple of months of the winter should be white ones in Wales and the Lake District. In Scotland, especially in the Cairngorms, snow persists from Christmas to Easter most years. In fact, the Scottish ski season depends upon such a length of stay.

Snow and ice add their own particular brand of excitement to a mountain walk. Easy summer paths can become extremely dangerous for unprepared parties. One Easter, several years ago, even the track alongside the Snowdon railway became almost impossible except in 'crampons'.

A few weeks earlier this would have mattered little as the only people on the mountain would have been climbers who would have quickly recognized the hazards involved; for the wind and sun had changed the snow into 'bubble ice', a surface that even a nailed boot finds difficulty with. However, because it was a fine Easter week-end many completely inexperienced 'day-trippers' attempted to reach the summit.

During that afternoon, sunshine changed to thick mist and three people were killed trying to return to the valley.

British mountains for all their lack of height can be very formidable given the right conditions. On that same week-end, a well-known Everest climber came across a party of scouts at the summit of Snowdon. The scouts – very wisely – had decided because of the mist to spend the night at the buildings at the top, rather than risk the descent.

Encouraged and guided by the famous climber they all roped up together, and set off down for Llanberis. After half an hour of groping about through thick mist and across frozen snow, the leader, still trying to follow the railway track down, disappeared over a cornice. Luckily he was held by the next scout on the rope, and hauled back into the land of the living. After a hasty consultation the party made their way back to the summit and spent a cold but safe night out in the coalshed of the deserted hotel.

To climb in snow conditions it will be necessary to invest in a further piece of equipment – an ice-axe. It is possible to buy a good metal axe for about £9, while a fibre-glass model will be priced at about £11. Choose an axe like you would pick a cricket-bat. Select a length and balance that suits your own height and build. It should be a short walking-stick length and not too heavy in the head. (*See* Fig. 27.)

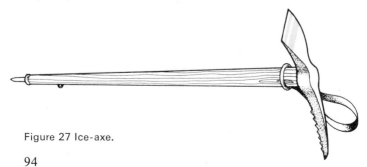

Figure 27 Ice-axe.

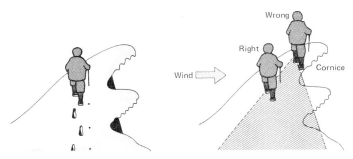

Figure 28 Traversing corniced ridges.

For the most part, on normal paths the axe will be used as a walking-stick – giving balance and support – when crossing deep and uneven snow.

With care most of the normal paths will 'go' in snow conditions, although until you have gained experience, routes that have steep ridges in them, or rock steps, should be avoided. (*See* Fig. 28.) Snow comes in many different varieties. Good snow – by a mountaineer's rating – is hard and compact. It needs a couple of good kicks with the toe of the boot before a step is made; an ice-axe can be pushed well down into it with difficulty, but once in will give a safe personal belay.

Under these conditions, a simple and normally boring grass slope of thirty-five degrees becomes an exciting pro-blem. Just as in rock-scrambling, the body is kept upright on snow slopes. Instead of picking out convenient footholds, steps are kicked in the snow. These should be big enough to get the sole of the foot into and should be spaced a foot or so apart. At each step the axe should be driven into the snow to give safety and steadiness as the next hold is made. (Figs. 29 & 30.)

As in summer, it is often easier to zig-zag up the slope and in this case the axe should be held in the hand nearest

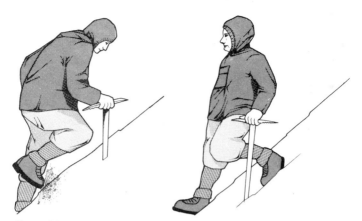

Figure 29 Kicking steps up
snow slope.

Figure 30 Descending snow
slope.

the slope, and again driven in at every stride. (Fig. 31.)
When the direction is changed it will be necessary to make a
larger step on the apex of the corner so that the body can be
turned round to face the new line of attack.

To look back at a set of steps going down below you is
very satisfying indeed. Just for a few days, perhaps just a
few hours, you have contributed something to the general
construction and texture of the mountain. A workmanlike
signature that can be seen from the valley below.

The ice-axe is used also as a brake, either in a controlled
'glissade' or in the event of a fall. This technique is one
which is best learned on the safety of a nursery slope. Find
a section of hard snow at a fairly steep angle with a good
run-out of soft snow below, then start practising the stop
some twenty feet/six metres from the bottom.

Opposite: Perfect winter conditions near the summit of
Cairngorm – hot sun, crisp snow and a party moving well
together.

Figure 31 Traversing snow slope.

Figure 32 Descending steep snow slope.

To work the brake it is necessary to press the pick of the axe gradually into the surface, applying more pressure bit by bit. A wild swing at the slope, using the axe like a pick, will probably snatch the axe out of the hand as it suddenly contacts the snow.

The correct technique is to grasp the axe by the head with one hand and by the shaft with the other. The body is kept well over the axe and the pick is gradually rotated to scratch into the slope; as the strain is taken by the arms more pressure can be used on the pick. (*See* Fig. 33.)

Although this movement is easy to do 'by arrangement', it is best to practise the technique until a fall can be checked from any initial position – whether it be head-first or sideways.

An hour or so of this sport will soon give you a healthy respect for gravity and a good idea of momentum!

On slopes of known length and quality, when the snow is

98

Figure 33 Stopping on hard snow.

Figure 34 Standing glissade.

fairly compact, it is possible to slide down at a fast but controlled speed. This is called glissading, and is good sport – when done properly.

The sitting glissade is like tobogganing without the sledge, the feet are lifted into the air and the more you lean back the faster you go. When the snow is harder, the feet can be used like small skis to plough down the slope. (*See* Fig. 34.) After a glissade the whole party is usually wet, with snow in their sleeves and boots and down their necks. For this reason this sort of exercise should be taken near the end of the day, when dry clothes are within sight.

But – once again – never, never, glissade down an unknown slope. Even during a few hours the texture of a slope can change, and where in the morning the snow was soft, by evening wind and sun can have changed it to bubbly ice. Remember that glissading when it gets out of hand can be too fast a means of descent.

A Different Environment

Wandering across the British hills in winter conditions, and these can occur from October to April, is a totally different game to the summer version.

This variation of climate is exaggerated by the vertical-factor. The difference in the micro-climate between the sheltered valley at 400 feet/122 metres above sea-level, and the wind-torn summits at 3500 feet/1066 metres is dramatic. The contrast between sunshine, cherry-blossom, and daffodils at the edge of the mountains and the world of biting winds, swirling snow and hoar-frost just above, has to be experienced to be believed.

If you misjudge the expected challenge of the day and set out in May-time gear for what turns out to be January bleakness – change your route to a low-level traverse before finding yourself committed to a snow-filled gully in gathering mist and freshening wind.

Don't become a statistic in the Mountain Rescue Annual Report.

8 Lightweight Mobile Camping

Although the greatest weight lifted by man is 4113 lb/ 1867·5 kg, achieved by the twenty-five-stone/159 kg French-Canadian Louis Cyr in a back lift off trestles, most of us would regard a fiftieth of this amount more than enough to move.

All around the world where conditions are unsuitable for wheeled transport, people carry heavy loads on their backs or on top of their heads. Many of these professional carriers shift large and heavy objects with amazing ease. They usually work in short bursts of speed, moving rapidly in between rests. In this way anything from a two-hundredweight/100 kg bale of rubber to a wardrobe is transported for short distances.

When longer distances are covered the weight is correspondingly smaller. The standard weight carried by the coolies on the approach march to Everest in 1953 was sixty pounds/27 kg, and twenty-five to thirty miles/forty to fifty kilometres were covered in a day. Higher up the mountain, where the air was thinner and the going more difficult, the Sherpa load was officially thirty pounds/13·5 kg, although often they managed fifty pounds/22·5 kg in emergencies.

You will not be many days into a walking and camping holiday before you find out what size of load still enables you to enjoy walking. I find that most people are happy with a little less than thirty pounds/13·5 kg on their back. A load heavier than this will soon bend most people double and limit their view of the passing countryside to a few square feet around their boots.

Consequently, we must budget in our mobile camping for our equipment and food to weigh less than thirty pounds/13·5 kg. This will dictate the 'cut of our cloth' and extra comfort or delicacies to eat will have to be accounted for on the scales.

I found personally that after several months of training I could include an air-bed in my load and still enjoy walking. The air-bed was more comfortable than cut bracken, but it weighed four pounds/1·8 kg and had to be carried all the way – while bracken often grew on the spot at the camp-site.

Before the war several enthusiasts belonging to various walking clubs had devised a load which apart from being very light in weight could be carried in the various pockets of a raincoat. Today the hardened specialist in bivouacking can keep his load within a dozen pounds/6 kg, and still keep dry and eat hot food twice a day.

The annual Karrimor Mountain Marathon – which is a race over fifty miles/eighty kilometres of mountain terrain with an overnight mountain camp, sees pairs of racers carrying less than twelve pounds/5·5 kg each and surviving above the tree-line in late October weather conditions. These teams are extremely experienced and sophisticated light-weight campers and have usually achieved lightness with little regard for cost.

The crux of the weight problem is the type of 'home' you intend to live in. It is this shell that will give you different degrees of comfort in camp and of heaviness on the march.

At one end of the scale there is the 'Everest' type tent with its sewn-in groundsheet and double-thickness walls, weighing as much as fifteen pounds/17 kg and costing up to £80. At the other end there is the domestic polythene wardrobe bag, six feet/183 cm long, weighing and costing very little.

Each shelter has its own advantages and is ideal in a certain circumstance. Obviously it would be pretty desperate trying to keep dry and warm at 4000 feet/1219 metres in mid-winter in the polythene bag, on the other hand life inside a closed-in 'Everest' tent would be grim on a hot still night anywhere.

Depending on what sort of camp you want is the type of cover you take with you. Generally speaking, British mountain camping falls into three groups:

1 Mountain camps in bad or doubtful weather
2 Low valley camps
3 One-night bivouacs in good weather

Each type of camp will demand different techniques and equipment.

The Mountain Camp

Once a tent is pitched above 2500 feet/750 metres in this country it becomes prey and fair game to every gale and storm that chooses to cross the Atlantic. In driving rain and wind no normal tent will stay water-proof. I have spent miserable nights in 'Everest' type tents on the slopes above 1400-foot/426-metre Llyn Llydaw, fighting unsuccessfully to stay dry. Yet the very tent that I was in had survived snowstorms at 23000 feet/7000 metres a few weeks previously!

Heavy rain by itself can be laughed at, as long as great care is taken to pitch the tent correctly, and the inside of the canvas is not touched while it is raining. Lashing rain is a different story. Flapping tent sides reduce the 'safe area' in the tent to an uncomfortable minimum, and often despite the most intense precautions the tent begins to leak. I have seen the two sides of the tent clap together after a particu-

103

A sheltered camp site high in the Cwm Glas at the 2000 feet (600 metre) level in Snowdonia.

larly vicious blast of wind, reducing in a second the tent's proofing to that of a sieve.

However, with luck, good pitching, a strong tent and reasonable weather a fair degree of comfort can be attained high up in the mountains all the year round.

The mountain tent is especially designed to stay where it is pitched and to this end it has thick guy-ropes and strong metal poles. It often has wide flaps sewn round the edge of the tent, which are usually weighted down with rocks to stop the wind getting underneath the tent. The groundsheet is sewn in and made of heavy duty plastic, while to complete the snugness, the double zipped door is protected by a deep hood and/or side awnings. The traditional sleeve-entrance is more effective in the really high mountains, where snow and not driving rain is the problem. (*See* Fig. 35.) However, the advent of really reliable zip-fasteners is helping the tent designer to offer adaptable entrances to suit all kinds of condition. A flysheet is absolutely vital when rain and wind are expected and it must reach right down to the ground and add a further peaked cap to the entrance if it is to really earn its keep. Remember that a flysheet can often weigh half as much as the tent, so it must do its job properly to be worthy of space on your pack.

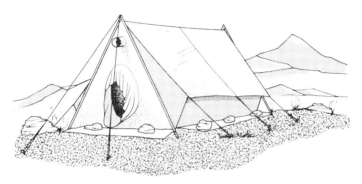

Figure 35 A mountain tent.

Many mountain tents now offer a wedge profile to reduce wind resistance. This is achieved by having an A-pole system at one end only and a single shorter pole at the other – usually the foot end. This shape is not so stable as the conventional ridge-shape but is well worth considering when selecting a tent.

If your camping is to be enjoyed in the insect season, then an insect netting door is highly recommended.

The fabric materials for the tent, flysheet and groundsheet need to be strong and tough. Cotton although heavier than proofed nylon can breath and avoids condensation within the tent. Nylon is certainly lighter than cotton but it is more expensive. It also doesn't absorb water so is easier

105

to carry when soaking wet. If the tent has good ventilation then you shouldn't wake up in the morning too damp. Cooking outside and keeping wet clothes in a plastic bag will also help keep things dry in a nylon tent.

Nylon also makes a noisy tent and can be difficult to pitch straight as the material stretches.

However, with all its disadvantages nylon is still a very respected material by back-packers and mountaineers, who are attracted to its lightness.

Many manufacturers offer tents in all kinds of combinations of materials, e.g. cotton inner and nylon flysheet. So you can decide what advantages you want and at what cost – to your pocket and your comfort.

The groundsheet must be sewn in. Here again we must balance weight against strength and length of life. A thin groundsheet is very vulnerable and a tent that is going to be used by several campers needs to have a durable floor.

A few of the many mountain tents that are available are noted below to give an indication of the range of cost:

1 Vango Force 10 Range Mk 3 Standard
   Two-man tent – cotton fly and tent – heavy-duty groundsheet. A-pole ridge design. Weight 13 lb 4 oz/6 kg. Price – about £50.

2 Bukta Andean
   Two–three-man tent – nylon fly and cotton inner. Two single poles ridge tent. Weight 9 lb/4·08 kg. Price – about £50.

3 Black's Arctic Guinea
   Three-man tent – 'Protex' cotton with cotton fly. Two A-poles ridge design. Weight 16 lb/7·26 kg. Price – about £70.

4 Marechal J3
   Two-man tent – nylon fly and cotton inner. Two single poles. Ridge design. Weight 13 lb/5·9 kg. Price – about £35.

The site for the high-mountain camp needs careful consideration. Ideal sites are few and far between. Usually it is necessary to compromise. A fine scenic position with a view will probably be in the wind, while soft turf grows only in hollows which become flooded in rain.

First of all look for shelter in a high camp-site. A small nook protected by a ten-foot/three-metre hump will do fine. Test the wind and then look for sheltered spots. If the weather looks doubtful and likely to change, it is from the west that the wind and rain will come, so make sure that your tent door is facing the rising sun. Wind usually blows strongest through gaps and across cols, but most peaks will have a pronounced leeward side if you look for it. A dead calm often exists just several feet below a windswept summit.

Some of the best sites are found at the entrance to a cwm; here amongst the terminal moraines the hummocks give good protection. The drainage is usually good and a clean stream usually flows into a small lake suitable for bathing. In the high camp-site there is seldom any problem with fresh water, as there is unlikely to be habitation above the tent. A quick check to make sure that the stream is running and that there is no dead sheep lying in it further up is all that is needed.

The Mountain Valley Camp

Although high altitude camping in all kinds of weather can be most exhilarating, for general satisfaction camping in a sheltered valley in the hills takes some beating. For a start, the risk of wind is reduced, and it is the wind combined with rain that spoils the quality of life when you are in a tent.

Consequently, the type of tent suitable for low-level camping can be less specialist in character than its roof-top cousin. This can ensure less weight and possibly lower cost.

The tent can be less of a 'cell' and more of a veranda. Doors can be wide and tie back completely; pegs and poles can be lighter; the flysheet less enveloping, and there is no need for snow-flaps.

However, with all these things said most of us who camp in the mountains have had experience of weather even in the most sheltered valley that is vicious. This means that we will be cautious about too many economies, especially if we camp outside the months of June, July and August.

Walking through the mountains and camping in the valleys is a great sport, and the possibility of keeping the tent weight down to around six pounds/2·7 kg makes the going greater.

Here are some well-tried models:

1 Black's Good Companion Standard
This two-man tent is a well-loved classic. A squared sheltering hood gives extra space. Weight 6 lb 8 oz/2·95 kg. Price – about £40.

2 Bukta Orienteer
A two-man tent – wedge-shaped. Weight 6 lb/2·72 kg. Price – about £40.

3 Saunders Dolomite
A two-man ridge suspended under a wedge-shaped flysheet which gives an extra storage area under cover. Weight 6 lb/ 2·72 kg. Price – about £50.

Don't rush into buying a tent. Have a good look round first. When you are out on the hills, take note of the various makes of tent that you see. A tent with dry and happy occupants is the best recommendation you can find.

There are plenty of camp-sites at a low level in the mountains. Down in the valleys the problem of wind will not be so great, and dry level patches are easily found.

But remember that the ingredients that make up a good camp-site also go to make up good grazing for sheep and cattle. The mountain farmer depends upon his few valley fields a great deal, and he has walled them in for a purpose. To avoid trouble and possible eviction go to the nearest farm when you have found a likely site, and ask his permission to camp. Most mountain farmers, particularly in remote areas, will never bother a camper who is on the top side of his 'mountain-wall', but will have genuine reasons for curtailing camping in their so very few and precious enclosed fields.

I have found that the majority of farmers are very sympathetic to and interested in mountain campers, as long as they are not put to any extra work or inconvenience by their presence. Study the Country Code and follow it carefully and you should pass the greatest test of camping – that you are welcome next time.

The 'golden rule' of all camping and especially mountain camping is to leave the site without any sign of your occupation. All tins, bottles and paper should be taken home again or down to the nearest official refuse bin. The empties will weigh less than on the way up, so they will be no real trouble. It is no real solution to bury rubbish under the nearest rock, for after a while – as has happened at some of the more frequented sites – every rock has a rotting pile of debris under it. So to bury rubbish it would be necessary to carry up a couple of rocks as well.

When rocks and large stones are used for holding down pegs and walls of tents make sure that they are piled up neatly on departure, and don't use a dry-stone wall as a quarry.

Be careful of the water supply in a valley camp. The farmer will be able to tell you about its suitability for drinking. Even if the main stream in a valley is unclean, there is usually a side tributary very close at hand that is safe. Try and keep the water clean and sweet. Do all the washing-up away from the stream or tarn's edge, then pour the greasy remains of a meal into a small hole dug in deep moss. Grease and bits of food spoil the look of a sparkling stream, especially if they belong to someone else camping above you.

At the end of a camp, the successful camper should be able to look over his shoulder at the site and see not one sign of his stay.

Bivouacking and Ultra-light Camping

Bivouac is a French word and is applied to a sparse night out in the Alps. Often returning climbers are caught out by night-fall while halfway down a mountain. Rather than struggle on and risk a fall in the dark a forced camp is made. This bivouac is a pretty sparse affair and the night is spent telling stories and slapping each other to stay awake and warm.

The planned bivouac is rather more comfortable and is used on a mountain face where it is necessary to take several days over the ascent, and where there is no room to pitch a tent. This kind of night out is also great fun in good weather, when even the confinement of a tent is an imposition.

On Alpine bivouacs down-filled jackets called 'Duvets' are worn, together with short bags for the legs called 'Pieds d'Eléphant'. These warm fittings covered by a wind- and water-proof sack give enough protection even above 10000 feet/3047 metres.

In this country, if the right nights are chosen, it is possible to spend some glorious hours out on the tops. A small hollow well filled with heather and a cloudless sky are all that is needed.

To keep off the dew some sort of covering is necessary, and a large plastic bag or light groundsheet will suffice for this. Many people find it difficult to sleep without something over their heads; their lack of ease is not caused by coolness but just by a feeling of being unprotected. A small hood erected over the head with a couple of sticks will help to cure this anxiety.

One of the best nights of my life was spent on top of the peak of Snowdon on Christmas Eve. Snug in a sleeping-bag tucked down in a hollow between two rocks, I dozed waiting for the sun to rise over the Carnedds. Whenever I woke I could see all the peaks around me in the moonlight. They were all black and white for the snow had come early that year. Below me the valleys were filled with grey masses of cloud, while above all the stars of the heavens pivoted in the sky. It was so still that I could hear the voices of a party 1500 feet/457 metres below me as they kicked steps up the snow. They were congratulating each other on being the only ones on the mountain.

An hour before dawn there were nearly twenty of us on top of the summit. We watched the stars fade into a grey background and suddenly the line of clouds in the east burst into an orange ridge and the rim of the sun climbed quickly up. Around us the hoar frost glowed pink in the sun and we followed the light down into the Llanberis valley for breakfast.

To have spent that night indoors, or even in a tent, would have been a tragedy.

The terrific interest now shown in long-distance travel through the mountains has helped develop some really efficient shelters weighing as little as three pounds/1·36 kg, which includes pegs, poles, groundsheet and flysheet.

These are all designed to keep one man in near comfort or two climbers in some discomfort – but warm and dry. These low-profile wedge-tents are ideal for those who travel the long-distance footpaths of Britain. The Pennine Way is 280 miles/450·5 kilometres long and often there is a need to camp when Youth Hostels are not available. Offa's Dyke on the Welsh Border is about 175 miles/282 kilometres in length and there are some beautiful camping opportunities on the way.

The best display and field testing of these ultra-light shelters is at the annual Karrimor Mountain Marathon race. This event, held in late October, is a fifty-mile/80·5 kilometre jog-trot across some rough area of upland Britain. There is an overnight camp at an exposed site and the competitors have to carry all they need on their backs for the complete journey.

Most of the tents used are single-skin nylon affairs – light but suffering from bad condensation problems unless the ventilation is well engineered. Those who take part in the Marathon have not only rationalized their gear to eleven pounds/5 kg each, but they have also worked out good tent discipline to enable them to spend the night in comfort.

The following tents have their enthusiasts:

1 The Karrimor Marathon – Mk II – two-man tent
   This is a simple design with twin front poles which gives a lot of space for the weight and money. The design lends itself to social camping as the tents can be attached to similar models to give a modular pattern. Weight 3 lb/1·36 kg. Price – about £40.

2 The Ultimate U.8
   A two-man bivouac tent. A sleeved alloy A-pole gives 3 ft 2 in/ 96·5 cm height at the entrance. Nylon ripstop upper. Weight 3 lb/1·36 kg. Price – about £25.

3 The SE-AB Okstindan
   A real quality featherweight which can even boast a flysheet and weighs only 3 lb 10 oz/1·65 kg. A peaked eve gives a protected doorway. Price – about £75.

The Sleeping-bag

A couple of blankets will often be sufficient for the odd night out at a base-camp in the valley, but for ease of carrying and greater warmth a proper sleeping-bag is essential.

This bag is made of stuffed quilting and is shaped like a sack that your entire body can disappear into. My first bag was made from an old bed quilt. It was filled with fair quality down and provided a good and cheap first bag – despite the Chinese dragon pattern on the cover.

Just as with the tents – money talks – and the best bag construction and fillings are the most expensive. There are three factors which govern the efficiency of a sleeping-bag:

1 The quality of the filling
2 The amount of the filling
3 The type of construction used in the making of the case

Goose-down is generally recognized as the finest filling available. The legendary 'Eider duck' down has long disappeared from the market – these past thirty years. Goose-down is practically stalk-free. It expands greatly and compresses to a very small volume. However, for such Rolls-Royce type filling you will have to pay over £60, and want the kind of protection necessary in the Himalayas.

Next in quality to goose is duck-down, and this is highly suitable for serious mountain camping in Britain all through the year. It is found in the middle-priced bags around the £30–£40 mark.

Cheaper natural fillings contain feathers, either curled or stripped off the stalk. Feathers do not fluff out well, in fact in cold weather chickens have to be kept indoors, so it would seem that feathers are not too good as insulators. So check your sleeping-bag before buying it – feel for stalks and if there seem to be many of them don't expect your bag to be useful when temperatures are below 10°C.

Most bags have a mixture of all the above materials in their fillings and this is done to save money and to give several good qualities to the bag. For instance, a top quality goose-down bag although giving maximum expansion – called 'loft' – also compresses under weight, so that although you are well insulated above your body you can be badly protected beneath. Such bags need to be used with a foam rubber or plastic camping mat, or have a certain amount of stiffer down added to the mix.

The case construction of the bag is also a matter of real importance to you. The cheapest natural filling bag is usually filled with curled feathers and is plain quilted, that is the two surfaces of the bag are stitched straight together. Obviously, this construction gives many cold spots along the line of stitching. (*See* Fig. 36.)

Wall quilting is used in the better bags, so that boxes are formed for the down and provided that there is enough down in each box this method gives good insulation all round.

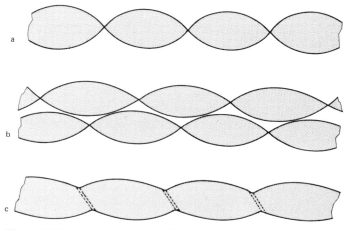

Figure 36 Sleeping bag construction: A Plain quilting – produces cold spots at lines of stitching; B Double quilting – cold spots eliminated and pockets of air retained for further insulation; C Allows good 'loft' of the filling and gives good insulation for minimum weight.

The most expensive bags are double quilted with the bulge of each section covering the weakness of its neighbour. There is the added advantage with this construction of air being trapped in between the layers as well.

Most bags are made of nylon material, but you should check the seams carefully and test if the material is too porous to hold in the down.

Well worth considering for the beginner are those sleeping-bags made with a Terylene or Dacron filling. These man-made fibres give quite good insulation, in fact they probably give you more protection when compressed under your hips and shoulders than the best down-filled bag. However, this attribute is a fault when you come to try and pack your bag into a rucksack. The man-made fibres are just that much more bulky. This packing difficulty apart, these artificial fibre bags are well worth the money at around £10.

While in camp turn your sleeping-bag inside out every morning, and hang it up to dry out. Before turning in at night, unroll the bag and lie on it for a while, this will give the down a chance to swell. For the sleeping-bag works on the same principle as does the 'layer of clothes'. Air is trapped in the feathers and is warmed by the body, thus keeping a thick layer of insulating air between the body and the surroundings. You will soon see how much a bag swells if you try to pack it back into its container soon after you get up in the morning.

An inner bag made out of an old sheet will help to keep the bag clean and fresh, as well as giving a little more warmth to the outfit.

When the bag is stored make sure that it is thoroughly dry before stacking it away at the back of a cupboard. In fact it is a good idea to use the bag as a quilt on your bed to ensure that it stays dry and moth-free.

Cooking Gear

Mountains are seldom covered with wood and trees. Most of them in this country are pretty bare of combustible material above the 1000-foot/304·5-metre contour. Therefore it will be very hazardous if you rely on local fuel to cook your supper. On occasions I have managed to collect enough heather and bilberry roots to start a fire with success, but it was a long job and needed dry conditions. In any case an open fire is dangerous near a tent, and will be very unpopular with farmers particularly in the hay season.

The small stove is by far the most convenient form of cooking. It is quick to light, gives good concentrated heat, can be shielded from the wind and usually weighs less than two pounds/900 g.

There are a dozen or so types of stove on the market today, burning paraffin, petrol, methylated spirits or some form of gas.

Although some of the gas-burning stoves are the lightest in weight, they need replacement cartridges every hour, and this can be a problem in out-of-the-way places.

For all-round reliability and ease of filling, the small half-pint paraffin or petrol stove takes some beating. On one filling they will burn for over an hour and can boil a pint/ 0·5 litre of water in under five minutes.

1 Primus $\frac{1}{2}$-pint paraffin stove
  Traditional model – cheap to use, efficient and cheerful. Weight 1 lb 14 oz/850 g. Price – about £10.

2 Svea $\frac{1}{3}$-pint petrol stove
  Needs no priming or pumping. Weight 6 oz/170 g. Price – about £9·50.

3 Karrimor Trangia methylated spirit stove
  Good design for preventing heat loss and comes with its own

saucepan and lid which can be used for frying. Weight 5 oz/ 142 g. Price – about £7·50.

4 Camping Gaz stove
Butane gas. Clean and convenient to use but expensive to operate. Also there is no indication of how much fuel remains in the can. Weight 2 lb 10 oz/1·19 kg. Price – about £3·50.

When you obtain a stove take good care of it. Keep it clean and make sure that it doesn't get dented. Before you take it away with you practise lighting it at home. With some experience you will soon become used to the stove's likes and dislikes. I found that with knowledge of one stove over a few months I could light it in the morning without waking up properly. This was a valuable skill and made early-morning tea a pleasure rather than a chore. It is important to carry petrol in a metal bottle and safer to keep paraffin and meths in alloy containers too.

With care and experience it is possible to use a stove inside a tent, and there is no more friendly sound in the world than that of a roaring stove at a high camp-site. A flat rock a foot square helps to keep the stove steady and safe from movements of the groundsheet.

Aluminium and polythene are the two standard materials used in mountain camping. A canteen set, consisting of a couple of deep pans and a lid, will be ample for two campers. Most mountain meals consist of boiled or fried preparations, and there is no point in carrying more than a few such containers when there is only one stove. Washing up, if considered necessary, can be done after each course.

It is often possible to 'borrow' several items of equipment from home to start your lightweight camping gear. There is usually a handleless small saucepan at the back of a cupboard and that with a deep aluminium plate and a plastic mug will be sufficient.

117

Try and make a collection of plastic containers, and then at the start of a trip transfer everything that is in cardboard or glass into them. You will then be crash- and storm-proof.

Rucksacks and Carrying Frames

Together with the food (*see* Chapter 9, Light-weight Food, pages 136–9) your gear will weigh some twenty-odd pounds/ 9 kg and to be effective has to be carried about somehow or other.

All over the world different races carry their loads in different ways. The Africans carry a load high on the head as did a Covent Garden porter. The Malays use a head-band which goes round the forehead and keeps the load high on the shoulders. The Chinese have long bamboo poles across their shoulders from which they hang things, using the same principle as a milkmaid's yoke. The Indian squaw carries her papoose in a cylinder high on her back.

Although they all look completely dissimilar they all do, in fact, use a common technique. The weight is taken high on the shoulders or head. This keeps the spine, which is the main strut of the body, underneath the weight, and so allows the body to work in its most advantageous position.

When we carry a heavy load ourselves we must follow the same basic principle, especially if we intend going very far. Bearing this principle in mind, anything which keeps the weight low down on the hips will soon tire us out. Many rucksacks are guilty of this fault. They allow the load to hang from the shoulders, instead of resting on them, and in many models it is on the hips that the sack rests. Again most rucksacks are wider at the bottom than at the top, which means that the weight of the load is always inclined to be in the wrong place – too low down.

When a load is heavier than about twenty-five pounds/

11·5 kg then it is best to have a frame to help distribute the weight properly and keep the sack from touching the back.

The design of a pack-frame has advanced greatly since the old 'Bergan' design, and the latest designs are based on the Yukon pack-frame. This piece of equipment presumably originated from the frame that the gold miners used in the 1890s. It was ideal for carrying awkward bundles and picks and shovels could be lashed to the outside.

The Lancashire firm of Karrimor have researched the design of high-loading packs and now offer five varieties of frame which are all highly recommended for the jobs they have to do. If you choose wisely there is no reason – other than growing out of the size – why your pack-frame shouldn't last a lifetime.

The drawing on page 120 shows the features of a good pack-frame. Apart from the basic design points and the strength of the joints, a good frame should be adjustable for your own personal dimensions. The Karrimor Tote-em Frame at about £9 is a good buy for the young climber.

With the frame it is necessary to buy a sack. Here it is possible to have a complicated sack with many pockets on the outside and divisions on the inside, or to settle for a plain sack with few trimmings. The enthusiastic back-packer seems to prefer the pockets, while the camper in the mountains makes do with stuffing all his gear into one large hole. However, if it is necessary to separate the gear inside the sack then nylon stuff-bags can be used – different colours for various categories of equipment.

When buying the sack consider the advantages of being able to use it without the frame. Often when using the sack as a suitcase on trains and buses, the rigid frame would be a nuisance and unnecessary. Check that the sack you buy can be used with the straps of the frame. Of course the

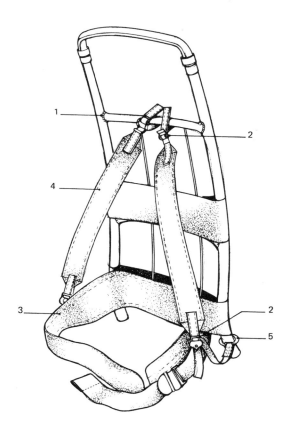

Figure 37 The Karrimor Orienteer pack frame.

Features to look for when selecting a frame:

1. Welded or strongly bolted/screwed joints
2. Harness adjustment
3. Wide hip-belt
4. Well padded wide shoulder harness
5. Facility for removing harness from frame so it can be used with the sack alone

120

Mountain weather is often wet, windy and cold. Here Lord Hunt ot Everest fame leads a group of young men dressed in strong anoraks and cagoules.

reverse is also true – your frame can be used without the sack for carrying anything from an oil drum to a tea-chest.

Packing the Gear

There are several important points to remember when packing a sack, which will help you and your gear to arrive at journey's end in good condition.

The first one is to keep the weight high up in the sack. This will mean that bulky but relatively light articles will go in first. The sleeping-bag is the obvious initial item to pack.

121

If you use an inner bag, put it into the down bag at home in the dry, for at the camp-site conditions might make it difficult to do the same job well.

Spare clothes should go in next – they need to be kept dry so should be deep down out of harm's way. A spare collection of matches, in an old aspirin bottle, is safe here too.

Next comes the food – all in plastic jars and bottles – and the cooking gear. The paraffin or petrol bottle will probably leak, no matter how good the stopper, so it had better be kept away from soft food, such as bread or bacon.

Lastly comes the tent, one of the heaviest pieces of equipment, and the first one needed at the camp-site. Make sure that the tent can be taken out of the sack without exposing anything to the weather. Nothing is more annoying than to watch all your possessions get soaked while the sack is turned inside out to find the peg-bag!

In the side-pockets or close at hand should be the various bits and pieces that will be needed on the journey. The first-aid kit, a spare pair of socks, maps and chocolate come in this group.

Get into the habit of always packing things in the same place and order – this will help you locate equipment in the dark, and will also help to avoid leaving anything behind.

9 Useful Information for the Mountaineer

The Weather: Official and Unofficial Forecasts

Bad weather doesn't 'stop play' in the sport of mountaineering, but it does tend to alter the rules of the game and make certain techniques more difficult.

The weather is an unfailing topic of conversation – and reputations are lost and made on the success of predicting 'tomorrow's weather'.

The official weather forecast that is given out for the various areas of the British Isles is as often wrong as it is right when applied to the mountains. Enthusiasts who listen eagerly and hopefully to the Friday night forecast must take 'a pinch of salt' when the newscaster says that, 'mainly fine weather is expected in Wales and the North of England'.

Mountains make their own weather and attract all the neighbouring clouds to help them do it. When I lived in Capel Curig – a small village 700 feet/213 metres up in Snowdonia – a common expression was, 'we're going down to the coast to see the sun'. Sure enough fifteen miles/twenty-four kilometres away it would be possible to bask in the sun while watching sombre clouds encircle the peaks we had left behind.

In general it is safe to say that the slightest hint of poor weather in an area forecast will mean rain in the mountains. Any mention of 'gale warning' in the Irish Sea will mean rough and wet weather in the mountains, for most of our 'bad' weather comes from the west.

Not only do certain mountain ranges make their own weather, but individual mountains within the range pick and choose what sort of day to have. Very often two valleys only a few miles apart will have widely varying weather on the same day. This change in the weather is so pronounced at times that it is possible to move from sunshine to rain in half a dozen strides.

With so many local variations, the official area forecast can – at its best – only be a general guide, your particular guide will be found among the farmers and villagers who live in the neighbourhood. These locals use all the weather-lore that countrymen all over Britain know, and add to it the locality's own peculiar signs.

Just as it is true that 'one swallow doesn't make a summer', it is also true that one cow lying down doesn't mean that it is going to rain.

It is an accumulation of signs that will help to predict a trend in the weather. For instance, if the climber is kept awake all night by 'shooting corns' and 'lowing cows', and watches in despair 'a pale haloed moon' followed by a 'red sunrise', he should be prepared for wet weather. (In any case he will not be fit to go very far, after that sort of night.)

But for all the signs – scientific or proverbial – it is best to remember the old farmer's advice when asked about the likelihood of rain. 'Rain, sir? Why I tell you it's not going to rain till the ground be wet: then we shall have plenty of it!'

For the weather, especially in the mountains, can change as often as the hour.

Weather Proverbs

> 'Hens' scarts and filly tails
> Make lofty ships carry low sails.'

124

An introduction to rope work using stances on an easy rock
face is a logical progression to scrambling and outcrop climbing.

'Trace in the sky the painter's brush:
The winds around you soon will rush.'

'Mackerel sky, mackerel sky:
Not long wet, not long dry.'

'Red sky at night, shepherd's delight;
Red in the morning, shepherd's warning.'

'Rainbow to windward, foul fall the day;
Rainbow to leeward, damp runs away.'

'If woollen fleeces spread the heavenly way,
Be sure no rain disturbs the summer day.'

'Wind dropping at sunset after storm,
Brings a morrow fine and warm.'

'When the swallows fly low,
Fine weather must go.'

'When the dew is on the grass,
Rain will never come to pass.'

'When the grass is dry at morning light,
Look for rain before the night.'

'Long foretold, long past
Short notice, soon past.'

'If the moon show a silver shield,
Be not afraid to reap your field;
But if she rises haloed round,
Soon we'll tread on sodden ground.'

'Clear moon,
Frost soon.'

'When the wind backs and the weather glass falls,
Then be on your guard against gales and squalls.'

'A coming storm our shooting corns presage,
Our aches will throb, our hollow tooth will rage.'

'When the wind's before the rain
Soon you'll make plain sail again;
When the rain's before the wind
Then your sheets and halyards mind.'

Lastly, here is an interesting table to keep your mind occupied while you huddle inside your tent watching the rain fall outside.

Probability of a Rainy Day
(*a*) After successive fine days

No. of Days	1	2	3	4	5	6	7	8	9
	%	%	%	%	%	%	%	%	%
Aberdeen	50	41	37	39	37	36	37	—	—
Kew	45	34	36	32	26	27	27	22	—

(*b*) After successive rainy days

No. of Days	1	2	3	4	5	6	7	8	9
	%	%	%	%	%	%	%	%	%
Aberdeen	67	70	76	70	66	67	72	75	78
Kew	56	61	61	64	64	67	73	69	70

A Mountaineer's Dictionary

Most places have names which describe their most important features. With a little knowledge of Welsh, Gaelic and Norse, it is possible to glean a fair amount of information about an unknown area by a study of its names on the map.

The following list contains many of the more familiar words and their meanings.

Aber (W & G) – Mouth of a river

Afon (W) – River

Allt (G) – Stream

Aran (W) – A grassy summit

Ard (G) – A high point

Arddu (W) – Pitch black

Bach (W) – Little, small

Bealach (G) – A pass, a gap

Beck (N.C.) – A brook

Bedd (W) – A grave

Beinn, Ben (G) – A mountain

Beudy (W) – A cowhouse

Bield (N.C.) – A shelter

Blaen (*pl.* Blaenau) (W) – high point, upper reaches

Bod (W) – Dwelling

Braich (W) – Arm

Brant (N.C.) – Steep

Bron (W) – Breast

Brwynog (W) – Rushy, marshy

Bryn (W) – Hill

Buachaille (G) – A herdsman

Burn (G) – A stream

Bwlch (W) – Pass

Cader (W) – Chair

Cae (W) – A field

Caer (W) – A fort

Cafn (W) – A trough

Cam (N.C.) – A ridge

Careg (*pl.* Cerrig) (W) – A stone, rock

Carnedd (W) – A heap of stones, cairn, hill

Cioch (G) – Breast

Clach (G) – A stone

Coch (W) – Red

Coed (W) – Wood, trees

Clogwyn (W) – A precipice

Coire (G) – Steep-sided hollow

G – Gaelic.   W – Welsh.   N.C. – North Country.

Craig (*pl.* Creigiau) (W) –
  Stone, rock
Crib (W) – A ridge, comb
Cwm (W) – A hollow, a valley
  head

Dearg (G) – Red
Dodd (N.C.) – A hummock
Druim (G) – A ridge,
  backbone
Drum (W) – A ridge, summit
Drws (W) – A door
Dwfr, dwr (W) – Water
Dyffryn (W) – Valley

Eas (G) – A waterfall
Edge (N.C.) – A narrow ridge
Esgair (W) – A shank, leg,
  ridge

Fach, fechan (W) – Small
Fawr (W) – Large
Feadan (G) – A narrow glen
Fell (N.C.) – A mountain
Ffynnon (W) – A spring
Force (N.C.) – A waterfall

Gallt (W) – A hill
Garbb (G) – Rough
Garth (W) – An enclosure
Ghyll (N.C.) – A steep valley
  with stream
Glan (W) – A bank, shore
Glas (G) – Green, grey watery
Glas (W) – Blue
Glyn (W) – A valley
Grind (N.C.) – A gate
Gwastad (W) – Flat
Gwyn (W) – White
Gwynt (W) – The wind

Hafod (W) – A summer
  dwelling
Hause (N.C.) – A ridge
Hen (W) – Old
How (N.C.) – A low hill, a
  burial mound

Inbhir (G) – A river mouth
Innis (G) – An island
Isaf (W) – Lower

Knott (N.C.) – A rocky edge

Lairig (G) – A long sloping
  pass
Llech (W) – A flat stone
Llithrig (W) – Slippery
Llyn (W) – A lake

Maen (W) – A stone
Mam (G) – Rounded hill
Man (N.C.) – A summit
Mawr (W) – Large
Moel (W) – A bare hill
Monadh (G) – A moorland
  mountain
Mor (G) – Large
Morfa (W) – A moor, marsh
Mur (W) – A wall
Mynydd (W) – A moorland
  mountain

Nant (W) – A brook, glen,
  gorge
Newydd (W) – New

Ogof (W) – Cave

Pant (W) – A hollow
Pen (W) – Head, top
Perfedd (W) – Middle

Pike (N.C.) – Peak
Pont, bont (W) – Bridge
Porth (W) – Gateway
Pwll (W) – A pool

Raise (N.C.) – Crest of a ridge
Rake (N.C.) – A gangway on
  a cliff
Rhaiadr (W) – A waterfall
Rhiw (W) – A slope, hill
Rhyd (W) – A ford
Rhos (W) – Moor, heath
Rigg (N.C.) – Ridge
Ruadh (G) – Red, reddish

Sarn (W) – A causeway
Scarth (N.C.) – A rocky
  outcrop
Sean (G) – Old, ancient
Sgurr (G) – A peak, conical
  sharp rock
Slape (N.C.) – Smooth,
  slippery
Sron (G) – A nose, peak,
  promontory

Stac (G) – A steep hill, conical
  rock
Stickle (N.C.) – A sharp peak
Suidhe (G) – A resting place

Taigh, Tigh (G) – A house
Tal (W) – End
Tarn (N.C.) – A mountain lake
Tri (W) – Three
Twll (W) – A hole, pit
Ty (W) – A house

Uachdar, auchter (G) –
  Upper ground
Uamh (G) – A cave
Uchaf (W) – Higher
Un (W) – One

Wyddfa (W) – A tomb,
  tumulus

Y, yr (W) – The
Yn (W) – In
Yspytty (W) – A hospice
Ystrad (W) – A dale

A Glossary of Mountaineering Terms

Conversation in the common rooms of the mountain hostels is always strongly spiced with 'technical jargon'. Descriptions of the day's adventures – half-truthful sometimes – are always amusing to listen to. The following list will help the non-climber understand what the 'line-shooting' is all about.

In general 'climbing talk' falls into two categories – the Understatement and the Exaggeration. Both it seems are designed to impress the listener. An account given in the first style will calmly call a howling gale a 'light breeze', or a deep bog – 'slightly wet underfoot'. At the other end of the

129

scale the 'exaggerator' will graphically describe a slight drizzle as 'a teeming monsoon', or a short section of scree as 'acres of vertical loose boulders'.

After serving an apprenticeship – during which time only nods of agreement or incredulous gasps are made – you will be able to take your pick of a style and join in the 'battle'.

Glossary

Abseil (or *Rappel*, or *Roping Down*).   A method of quick descent down a rock-face by using the rope double and sliding down it. (This is the fastest method of descent apart from one obvious exception.)

Arête.   A narrow ridge leading up to the summit and usually made of bare rock.

Artificial aid.   The use of pitons and double-rope technique.

Backing-up (or *Chimney-ing*, or *Bridging*).   A method of ascending a wide crack with the back pressed against one wall and the feet on the other.

Belay.   To fasten the rope round a projection of rock in such a way as to make fast the climber to the stance. As a noun it is used to describe the actual anchorage that is used.

Buttress.   A mass of rock projecting from the mountain upon which rock-climbing routes are usually found.

Chimney.   A narrow gully that is wide enough to bridge across, usually vertical.

Chockstone.   A rock or stone that is jammed in a crack, allowing a rope to be passed behind it to make a belay.

Col.   A high pass or gap between two peaks.

Combined Tactics.   A method in which the second climber allows himself to be used as a ladder to enable the leader to surmount an obstacle.

Cornice.   A term borrowed from architecture, indicating an overhanging mass of snow formed at the crest of a ridge.

Crack.   A narrow chimney that is too small to get the body into, but in which an arm, hand or foot can be wedged.

Diff. The abbreviation of Difficult, a term of degree of hardness in rock-climbing. The range is: Easy, Moderate, Difficult, Very Difficult, Severe, Very Severe, Exceptionally Severe. All rock-climbs are assessed in one of these categories.

Etrier. A short rope ladder, used in artificial climbing.

Exposure. A climb is said to be exposed when the situations on it are airy. Plenty of 'daylight' underneath a move can increase its apparent difficulty.

Faith and Friction. A term applied to progress on steep, holdless slabs.

Gardening. The process of cleaning out a climb to find the holds.

Gendarme. A tower or pinnacle dominating a ridge and making an obstacle to progress.

Gully. A ravine on the mountainside, usually with a stream in it, and surrounded by steeper rocks.

Jammed Holds. A method of wedging a hand, finger or fist into a crack to make a grip.

Karabiner (or *Snap Link*). A steel or alloy oval with a gate in one side. It is used for attaching the rope to belays. (Slang – 'a crab'.)

Knitting. The mass of tangled climbing rope.

Layback. A very strenuous method of climbing a crack. The hands pull while the legs push.

Leader. The first man on the rope.

Peel-off. To fall or jump off a climb.

Pitch. A section of a rock-climb that is done at one run-out of rope.

Piton (or *Peg*). A metal spike with an attached ring, or with a hole in it. It can be hammered into rock cracks or into ice, and used as a belay.

Rib. A minor ridge of bare rock.

Running Belay (or *Runner*). A device for safeguarding the leader. The rope runs through a karabiner which is attached to a sling belay.

Slab. Flat masses of rock lying at angles less than the vertical.

Slack. The un-tight rope between the leader and second man, or between any two climbers.

Stance. A place where a climber can belay himself and bring up the next man.

Thank-God-Hold. A fine hand-hold found at the end of a difficult section of climbing.

Useful Organizations

Sports Council

Is a Royal Chartered body which concerns itself at national and regional levels with all sport, outdoor and recreational activities. The Sports Council maintains the National Mountaineering Centre – Plas-y-Brenin at Capel Curig, North Wales. At this Centre courses are organized for the public, young and old, in all forms of adventurous outdoor activities – mountain-walking, rock-climbing, camping, environmental studies and skiing. Most of the courses are of one week duration and the cost including the hire of boots and other necessary equipment is seldom more than £32. The Centre has a residential staff of instructors, all experts in one form or another of outdoor activity, who teach on the various courses. On the standard Introductory Outdoor Activity Course no previous experience is required and everything is explained from first principles.

Information about Plas-y-Brenin and other Sports Council courses can be obtained from – The Sports Council, 70 Brompton Road, London SW3 1EX.

Scottish Sports Council

Courses on outdoor activities are organized by the S.S.C. particularly at their fine Centre in the Cairngorms called Glenmore Lodge, near Aviemore. Ski mountaineering and winter snow work are specialities of this Centre.

Field Studies Council

Encourages field work and research in such subjects as botany, zoology, geography, natural history and archaeology. All these activities are practical studies that many mountaineers have a great interest in. The Council runs several centres around the U.K.

Further information from – The Field Studies Council, Preston Montford, Montford Bridge, Shrewsbury SY4 1HW.

Outward Bound Schools

These schools are set up in various wild parts of Britain. Courses for girls (over $14\frac{1}{2}$ years) and boys (over 14 years) are fairly strenuous and last for one month. The mountain-based schools base their work on climbing and back-packing, while the sea schools tend to concentrate on sailing and seamanship. Details of the courses available can be obtained from – Outward Bound Trust, 34 The Broadway, London SW1H 0BQ.

Youth Hostels' Association

Administer a chain of 300 hostels throughout the U.K., most of them situated in the areas that interest the climber and rambler. The Y.H.A. also arranges courses in climbing and general mountaineering at several of their hostels – Adventure Holidays for those over the age of 16.

Details of membership with reciprocal rights in Scottish hostels are available from – The Y.H.A., Trevelyan House, St Albans, Hertfordshire. In Scotland – Scottish Y.H.A., 7 Glebe Crescent, Stirling, FK8 2JA.

Ramblers' Association

The objects of the Ramblers' Association are to encourage rambling and mountaineering to foster a greater knowledge, love and care of the countryside and to work for the preservation of natural beauty, the protection of footpaths and the provision of access to open country.

Details of area and group addresses can be obtained from – The Ramblers' Association, 1/4 Crawford Mews, York Street, London W1H 1PT.

British Mountaineering Association

Now has the resources to concern itself with all aspects of climbing – expeditions, access, technique courses, equipment testing and club structure. Information from – The B.M.C., Crawford House, Precinct Centre, Booth Street East, Manchester 13. Official comment by the B.M.C. Secretary is published in *Climber and Rambler Magazine*.

Mountaineering Literature

Most libraries will be found to possess a dozen or more books on climbing and mountaineering. Many of the books will be old and out-of-date, but among these old books are several classics, which every climber should read. These books are the volumes that fill in the history of the sport.

More recent books will either be of a technical nature, or narrative works, describing expeditions in this country, the Alps and the Himalayas.

The following list contains some of the more important and readable books which will delight in the winter evenings. Given the right book, the 'armchair' mountaineer can make some glorious ascents.

Mountain Craft, by G. Winthrop Young. Methuen.
This book is considered to be the standard work on mountaineering. It is comprehensive and easily read.

Mountaineering, by Alan Blackshaw. Penguin Books.
A most comprehensive catalogue of climbing techniques and terminology.

On Climbing, by Charles Evans. Museum Press.
A blend of personal recollection, ranging from the Welsh Berwens to the Himalayas, and technical advice for beginners and experts.

Let's Go Climbing, by C. F. Kirkus. Nelson.
A very readable book which gives advice on elementary rock-climbing and mountaineering.

Scrambles Amongst the Alps, by Edward Whymper. John Murray.
A classic which has still the power to thrill with its account of the first ascent of the Matterhorn.

My Climbs in the Alps and the Caucasus, by A. F. Mummery. Blackwell's Mountaineering Library.
Describes the pleasures and penalties of mountaineering in enthusiastic style. Another classic.

The Romance of Mountaineering, by R. L. G. Irving. Dent.
A well-written book dealing with the philosophy as well as the technique of mountaineering.

Climbs and Ski Runs, by F. S. Smythe. Blackwood.
The best of several well-written books by this author

Upon that Mountain, by Eric Shipton. Hodder and Stoughton.
A narrative that ranges across the large mountains of the world.

Memoirs of a Mountaineer, by F. Spencer Chapman. Reprint Society.
A narrative of a mountaineer's progress from Helvellyn to Himalaya, and an account of Lhasa – the Holy City.

Annapurna, by Maurice Herzog. Jonathan Cape.
A thrilling account of the first ascent of an 8000-metre peak.

The Ascent of Everest, by John Hunt. Hodder and Stoughton.
A textbook on expedition management, combined with a description of an historical event.

Climbs of my Youth, by André Roch. Lindsay Drummond.
Accounts of some of the hardest climbs in the Alps.

Starlight and Storm, by Gaston Rebuffet. Dent.
A remarkable book which tells of the ascents of eight major routes in the Alps.

Mountaineering in Scotland, by W. H. Murray. Dent.
A fascinating book full of the mountaineering spirit, and describing winter and summer ascents in Scotland.

Climbing Days, by Dorothy Pilley.
Gives an insight into the thrill of climbing and the fun of being in the hills.

Nanga Parbat, by Karl Herrligkoffer. Elek Books.
Containing an account of Hermann Buhl's solo ascent of the mountain after a night out at 26000 feet/7921 metres.

I Bought a Mountain, by T. Firbank. Harrap.
A best-seller of life on the Glyder mountains of Wales.

The Mountaineer's Week-end Book, by Showell Styles. Seeley Service.
Mingles entertainment with instruction and facts for the mountaineer.

Mountain Leadership, by Eric Langmuir. Scottish Sports Council.
An excellent and authoritative booklet on all aspects of mountaineering in the U.K. in summer and winter. Required reading for all those taking their Mountain Leadership Certificate.

Expedition Guide, by John Disley. Duke of Edinburgh's Awards.
A good check-list on all aspects of mountain expedition work in British hills in summer time.

Safety on Mountains, the handbook of the B.M.C. and required reading for all those who go to the hills.

Lightweight Food

Unless the camper has the makings of a chef in him, he is unlikely to rise gastronomically much above boiling and frying. With only one primus stove, a limited amount of fuel

A free abseil over a nose of rock, using the classical method.

and a few containers, the lightweight camper is concerned with foods that are quickly cooked and sustaining.

He will expect, if he is sensible, his food – like the rest of his equipment – to be light. Most foods have a certain amount of water content in them. Some vegetables are comprised almost entirely of water. Water is the one commodity of which there is usually an abundance in the mountains, therefore dehydrated powders and mixtures are ideal for camping.

The following table shows the great difference in weight:

	lb	oz		lb	oz
Tin of soup (1 pt)	1	2	Soup packet		2
Bottle of milk (1 pt)	2	6	Milk tube		4
Potatoes	1	8	Potato powder		5
Mixed vegetables	1	8	Dried vegetables		2
Bread	2		Oatmeal biscuits		8
Meat (fresh)	3–4		Corn-beef	1	
Fresh fruit	3–4		Dried fruit		8
	15	8		2	13

These foods have the added advantage of being packed in tinfoil and polythene, which gives a much higher ratio of food to package.

The prices are much the same for most of the two types of food. On milk, potatoes, meat and bread you will have to pay a little more for the privilege of a light pack.

Toothpaste type tubes for milk, tomato purée and even cheese, are ideal for the peripatetic camper – with the cap screwed on a half-used tube can be packed with impunity, whereas opened bottles and jars are certain trouble in a travelling rucksack.

With all the foods that need to be re-constituted with water, give them plenty of time to soak. In fact, 'putting the veg to soak' should be one of the first jobs done at camp. Most preparations respond more urgently to hot-water baths.

Two meals during the day – breakfast and supper – should be hot meals with a high calorific and protein value.

Sample menus would be as follows:

Breakfast Porridge (try it uncooked – it's first-class) with hot milk and sugar and salt.

Bacon and scrambled egg (dried egg). Bacon fried in butter.

Biscuits with butter and dried fruit.

Coffee or tea.

Supper   Soup.

A stew – with mixed vegetables and dried meat, thickened with potato powder.

Biscuits and butter with cheese, and fruit.

Coffee with milk and sugar.

These are simple meals, but contain all the essentials for a balanced diet and are easy to prepare and cook.

At the right time of year, nature opens her own larder door, and it is possible to supplement supplies with on-the-spot fresh food.

Bilberries often cover mountain slopes. These small, dark-blue berries grow on thin smooth-stemmed plants, and are often hidden by the many leaves which surround them. Eaten raw or stewed and served with condensed milk and sugar they make a perfect end to a mountain meal.

Blackberries grow at lower levels, and will be found in profusion on broken-down walls and in thickets. A pound of these will set your vitamin 'C' rating sky-high for a few days. Try saving some for breakfast and mixing them with the uncooked oatmeal, sugar and milk.

Cowberries ripen late on Scottish hills. These 'red whortle-berries' are too tart to eat raw, but stewed and sweetened make an excellent dish – much favoured in Norway.

Mushrooms – easily recognized from other fungi – do sometimes grow on mountain fields. But the 'local' using prior knowledge will probably beat you to the morning's picking.

For many other 'hedgerow' delicacies a good book on edible fungi and herbs will help you search for free food.

The Art of Hitch-hiking

If you are in no hurry to reach your destination and have no definite time-table to keep to, travel on the roads by begging lifts is a distinct possibility. Even the mountaineer who can afford to always travel by train will often find that he must use the road to complete the last twenty miles/thirty-two kilometres or so to the mountains. Railheads are usually well short of the higher valleys.

Hitch-hiking is first and foremost a cheap method of travelling, but it is also a very uncertain form of transport. The hitch-hiker must expect to spend many nights out, dozing in the hedgeside at some lonely cross-roads, waiting for the early morning milk lorries and post-office vans.

I still recall, whenever I pass the spot, a frosty February night spent in the middle of a grassy roundabout near Wellington on the A5. Wrapped up in my sleeping-bag I shared the night on the 'island' with one oak tree and four keep-left signs.

The hitch-hiker is not a rare figure on most British roads. Consequently, those mountaineers who wish to travel 'by the thumb' must expect a fair amount of competition, especially on Friday nights near the outskirts of any large city.

Common sense and psychology must be used to win a place in a car or a perch on the back of a lorry. The following points are well worth considering:

1 *Appearance*

Always look tidy and as presentable as possible. Comb your hair and keep your face clean. Look cheerful and as if you will be interesting company for the driver.

Stay dry. No driver will want a sodden passenger in his

car. An umbrella will not only keep off the rain but will add to your interest value. A climbing rope round the shoulders and an umbrella furled or up are sure-fire lift-getters.

Keep your gear dry and as small as possible, consistent, that is, with not being expected to walk 200 miles/282 kilometres with it.

2 *Numbers*

The lone figure standing at the side of the road is likely to receive the necessary sympathy from the driver, and is likely to strain his engine but little. So unless there is some good reason for keeping in a party always split up into individuals. A 'drawing of straws' is a good way of deciding who stands still and who walks on to the next good spot.

Girls should never travel in groups less than two in number. This is not such a handicap as they do bring out the 'gallant knight' quality in most drivers.

They should never travel after dark by this method.

3 *Stance*

Firstly – always make your intention perfectly clear. Stand still, face the oncoming traffic and use your arm and thumb vigorously for as long as you can see the 'white of the number-plate'.

Smile – even if obviously ignored. In fact, a polite wave of recognition to the driver's disinclination to stop will often produce the required lift.

Make sure that the driver can see your face. At night stand under a light so that your face is lit up.

4 *Position*

Find a good strategic spot and stay there.

Make sure that you are not half a mile before an important cross-roads. No driver likes to stop and then find that he can be of little help.

Don't expect a heavy vehicle to stop on a hill.

Don't expect any vehicle to stop on a bend, especially if the road is narrow.

Find a natural slowing-down spot where the road is flat and wide and there is good visibility. The driver will need time to sum you up. The end of the 30 m.p.h. limit, or thirty yards/twenty-seven metres on from a main cross-roads or roundabout are usually good situations.

5 *The Route*

Carry a road map with you and be prepared to make a lightning decision when offered an alternative to the route you had in mind. When in doubt, particularly at night, keep to main roads, even if it means foregoing several more miles in your general direction but on minor roads. You may have a long walk on desolate lanes to regain the night life of the main trunk road.

6 *Attitude on stopping the Driver*

As soon as it is obvious that you have hooked a car or lorry, pick up your gear and sprint smartly after it. Be polite and tell him your general aim. If you decide against taking his short-haul lift, and it is often foolish to leave a first-class position for anything short of the next town, thank the driver profusely and leave him in a state of mind that he will stop for a subsequent hitch-hiker.

142

If your lift is a good one, ask the driver where he would like you to put your rucksack. Be very careful stowing your gear, watch the door surrounds with the metal frame of the sack, and the roof lining with that ice-axe. Be careful of your boots on the carpet – in fact nailed boots are sometimes a powerful deterrent to a successful hitch-hiking career.

If you are put up on the back of a lorry make sure that you have agreed on your putting-down point before the Perkins diesel engine starts up. I once beat on the roof of the cab for ten off-the-route minutes before the driver heard me at all.

Once the lift starts be a conversationalist. The driver probably picked you up, not out of compassion, but for company's sake. Don't let him down. Tell him your plans, let him know how he has fitted into the general plan of getting you to your journey's end. Keep him amused. Listen considerately to his views on climbing – its value and its foolhardiness. Don't disagree too vigorously. Remember that you are a guest.

Congratulate him on the sound of the car's engine, its performance up hills and the general condition of the body-work – unless it is obvious that such comments might be mistaken for sarcasm.

With tact and enthusiasm miracles can be worked. A driver enjoying your company will often go out of his way to help you on yours, while there are reports of lunches and dinners received *en route*! Successes like these will be a real compliment to your ability as a hitch-hiker.

7 *Finally*

At all times remember that it is you who are looking for the favour. No one owes you a lift – be thankful when one is given.

The Country Code

The countryside in Britain is, for the most part, more like a garden than a wilderness. It is farmed and afforested over most of its area. Even on mountains, heaths and marshes the land is used as much as possible for cultivation and grazing for animals.

Please remember!

Guard Against All Risk of Fire
Fasten All Gates
Keep Dogs under Proper Control
Keep to the Paths across Farm Land
Avoid Damaging Fences, Hedges and Walls
Leave No Litter
Safeguard Water Supplies
Protect Wild Life, Wild Plants and Trees
Go Carefully on Country Roads
Respect the Life of the Countryside

People who have knowledge of the country and country ways respect the countryman's way of life, leave his things alone, and do nothing to interfere with his work or his belongings.